W9-AQB-152

# The
# Affective
# Domain
# in Education

## Thomas A. Ringness
UNIVERSITY OF WISCONSIN

# The Affective Domain in Education

**Little, Brown and Company**
Boston · Toronto

Library of Congress Catalog Card No. 74-26406

THIRD PRINTING

*Published simultaneously in Canada
by Little, Brown & Company (Canada) Limited*

Printed in the United States of America

*Illustrations by Mary J. Gander*

TEXTUAL ACKNOWLEDGMENTS

*Epigraphs*

*Pages v–vi:* "The Calf Path." Reprinted by permission of Lothrop, Lee & Shepard Co., Inc. from *Dreams in Homespun* by Sam Walter Foss.
*Page 19:* From "The Contribution of Developmental Psychology to Education — Examples from Moral Education," *Educational Psychologist,* 10 (1973), 13. Copyright © 1973 by APA Division 15. Reprinted with permission.
*Page 59:* From *The Brothers Karamazov* by Fyodor Dostoyevsky, translated by Constance Garnett (New York: Random House, 1950). Reprinted with permission.
*Page 80:* From *Concern* 1 (1971), 2.
*Page 96:* From "Value Education in the Social Studies," *Phi Delta Kappan,* 50 (1969), 457–61. Reprinted with permission.
*Page 121:* Lines of poetry from "Tomlinson" in the book *Rudyard Kipling's Verse:* Definitive Edition. Reprinted by permission of Mrs. George Bambridge and Doubleday & Company, Inc.
*Page 134:* From "Humanizing the Humanism Movement," *Phi Delta Kappan,* 55 (1974), 401. Reprinted with permission.
*Page 155:* From the play *Back to Methuselah* in *The Works of George Bernard Shaw* (London: Constable & Company, 1930), p. 7. Reprinted with permission of The Society of Authors on behalf of the Bernard Shaw Estate.

*The publisher is also grateful to the following persons:*

AMERICAN BROADCASTING COMPANY   For permission to summarize the news documentary *Eye of the Storm,* first broadcast 11 May 1970.
AMERICAN PSYCHOLOGICAL ASSOCIATION   For permission to quote from D. S. Meichenbaum, "Examination of Model Characteristics in Reducing Avoidance Behavior," *Journal of Personality and Social Psychology,* 17 (1971).
DEMBAR EDUCATIONAL RESEARCH SERVICES, INC.   For permission to adapt the table "Flanders' Interaction Analysis Categories" from N. A. Flanders, "Interaction Analysis and Inservice Training," in Klausmeier, H. J., and O'Hearn, G. T.

(eds.), *Research and Development Toward the Improvement of Education* (1968).

EDUCATIONAL PSYCHOLOGIST   For permission to quote from L. Kohlberg, "The Contribution of Developmental Psychology to Education — Examples from Moral Education," *Educational Psychologist*, 10 (1973). Copyright © 1973 by APA Division 15. Reprinted with permission.

NED A. FLANDERS   For permission to adapt the table "Flanders' Interaction Analysis Categories" from "Interaction Analysis and Inservice Training," in Klausmeier, H. J., and O'Hearn, G. T. (eds.), *Research and Development Toward the Improvement of Education* (Madison, Wis.: Dembar Educational Research Services, 1968).

JACK R. FRAENKEL   For permission to quote from "Value Education in the Social Studies," *Phi Delta Kappan*, 8 (1969).

HARPER & ROW, PUBLISHERS, INC.   For material adapted from Chapter 11 in *Motivation and Personality*, 2nd Edition, by Abraham H. Maslow. Copyright © 1970 by Abraham H. Maslow. By permission of Harper & Row, Publishers, Inc. Also for permission to quote from H. J. Klausmeier and W. Goodwin, *Learning and Human Abilities*, 2nd ed. (1966).

LAWRENCE KOHLBERG   For permission to quote from "The Contribution of Developmental Psychology to Education — Examples from Moral Education," *Educational Psychologist*, 10 (1973).

CHARLES E. MERRILL PUBLISHING CO.   For permission to paraphrase from L. Raths, M. Harmin, and S. B. Simon, *Values and Teaching* (1966).

NEW YORK UNIVERSITY EDUCATION QUARTERLY   For permission to quote from B. F. Skinner, "The Free and Happy Student," *New York University Education Quarterly* 4, No. 2 (1973).

BOARD OF TRUSTEES, OBERLIN COLLEGE   For permission to paraphrase from Carl R. Rogers, *On Becoming a Person* (Boston: Houghton Mifflin, 1961). © 1954 by the Board of Trustees of Oberlin College.

PHI DELTA KAPPAN   For permission to quote from J. R. Fraenkel, "Value Education in the Social Studies," *Phi Delta Kappan*, 8 (1969).

RANDOM HOUSE, INC.   For permission to quote from T. A. Ringness, *Mental Health in the Schools* (1968). © Copyright, 1968, by Random House, Inc.

LOUIS E. RATHS   For permission to paraphrase from L. Raths, M. Harmin, and S. B. Simon, *Values and Teaching* (Columbus, Ohio: Chas. E. Merrill, 1966).

JEAN M. SULLIVAN   For permission to quote in entirety the article "Wanted: Soft Revolutionaries," *Karma*, 24 May 1973.

WISCONSIN STATE DEPARTMENT OF PUBLIC INSTRUCTION   For permission to quote from DPI Code 3.03 (1b).

SCHOOL OF EDUCATION, UNIVERSITY OF WISCONSIN   For permission to quote from the proposal submitted by the School of Education to the Department of Public Instruction for implementing human relations requirements.

XEROX FILMS   For permission to summarize the ABC news documentary *Eye of the Storm*, first broadcast 11 May 1970. Distributed by Xerox Films, Middletown, Ct.

# PREFACE

One day through the primeval wood
A calf walked home as good calves should;
But left a trail all bent askew,
A crooked trail as calves all do.

A dog took up the trail next day.
A bear, too, went along the way.
And then a wise bellwether sheep
Pursued the trail o'er vale and steep.

And drew his flock behind him too
As good bellwethers always do.
And from that day, o'er hill and glade
Through those old woods a path was made

And many men wound in and out
And dodged and turned and bent about.
And uttered words of righteous wrath
Because 'twas such a crooked path.

The forest path became a lane
That bent and turned and bent again.
And this, before men were aware,
Became a city's thoroughfare.

*And soon the central street was this*
*Of a renowned metropolis.*
*A hundred thousand men were led*
*By one calf near three centuries dead.*

*For men are prone to go it blind*
*Along the calf paths of the mind*
*And work away from sun to sun*
*To do what other men have done.*

*They keep the path a sacred groove*
*Along which all their lives they move;*
*But how the wise wood gods laugh*
*Who saw the first primeval calf.*

— SAM WALTER FOSS

This short poem by Sam Walter Foss contains something like a sermon for teachers, parents, and psychologists. It refers to the role of tradition in governing behavior; to our lack of questioning "established truths"; and to our frequent lack of creativity and exploration of new ideas and ways of behaving. We can read into it implications concerning our propensity for accepting a mediocre or even inadequate status quo rather than engaging in problem-solving. We may think of our tendency to accept old attitudes and values rather than to question them and perhaps find new ones. Possibly it is not only simpler, but safer, not to question authority or to be "different," even if being different might be better. For at least if a path exists, we know someone has travelled there before; but if we form a new path, we cannot be certain where we will arrive.

If we look around us we can see the importance of imitation in governing behavior, the importance of chance experiences in determining ways of life. We can see some youths who still employ outworn behaviors which they learned as children, and some adults, too, who act from habit, conforming to immature patterns of living that are no longer useful to them. Unfortunately, rigidity — hence inefficiency, conflict, and frustration — may persist among these people for many years, while early learning and behavior goes unquestioned. Such ineffectual behavior can be passed on through many generations, so that today's children are in part the victims of ways of looking at life which their parents learned from their grandparents. Not only may children completely fail to consider the effect of cultural changes and progress on the usefulness of traditional

attitudes and values; they may perpetuate attitudes that never were useful.

On the other hand, it would be difficult for each generation to develop its attitudes and values and ways of behaving completely anew. It would be inefficient for each generation to rediscover the wheel. "The Calf Path" does provide food for thought, though. Where can we go from there?

The affective domain contains the feelings or emotional components of our lives. Thus positive and negative feelings, as well as emotionally toned attitudes, values, interests and appreciations, morals and character, and even personal and social adjustment fall within that domain. Thus affective learning plays an important part in a young person's development.

Yet affective learning, although it has not been completely neglected in the schools, has been slighted. There are reasons for this, of course. For one thing, although courses may have affective objectives, over time they tend to erode (Krathwohl et al., 1956). This may be partly because it is difficult to evaluate the attainment of affective objectives. But furthermore, philosophical and perhaps political and legal difficulties are involved in evaluating pupils' attitudes and values, especially if such evaluation leads to grading and marking. Fear of indoctrination and a belief that democracy implies freedom of choice are factors. Another cause of erosion may lie in the frequently slow attainment of affective objectives, which are usually developed over time (Kohlberg, 1973).

Still, many of our social problems might be solved, or at least minimized, if pupils learned to think through what they believed and became committed to their values. To this end, we need to consider both the attitudes that we purposely foster in the schools *and* those which we unwittingly foster. The fact that attitudes and values are learned presents us with our greatest hopes for the future. We can help children to learn and to explore, to seek ways of behaving that will satisfy them as individuals, as well as satisfy and improve society. Inadequate or maladaptive behavior can be corrected. New, more useful behavior can be encouraged. We need to help children to understand themselves better, to understand others, to determine how they feel, how they got that way, what alternatives they can muster, and to project the consequences of their feelings and points of view. The importance of doing so is the subject of the first chapter of this book.

Affective learning is discussed in most educational psychology textbooks, but usually only in chapters on "motivation," "emotions," "attitudes and values," and "personal and social adjustment." Most such books are also written from a particular theoretical point of view. I hope that this book will integrate some of the concerns of the affective domain, as well as show how affective behavior is learned and may therefore be modified. To that end Chapter 2 deals in some detail with a definition of the field; various points of view are set forth. Both the learning-theory approach and the humanistically oriented approach are enlarged on in succeeding chapters: Chapters 3 through 6 treat the affective domain from the rather traditional, learning-theory orientation; Chapters 7 and 8 reflect the humanistic point of view. These outlooks, although antithetical, can be used together in the school setting if the teacher does not take an extreme position. Chapter 9 discusses helping the teacher to become more "affective." Throughout the book, the research upon which the text is based is presented. Practical suggestions and implications for the teacher are paramount, however.

The material in this book has been tried in several university courses in educational psychology. Both students and faculty were asked to evaluate early versions; the present material is an attempt to make use of their evaluative comments. No prior study of psychology has been assumed; the material should therefore be appropriate for beginning students in educational psychology. For the more advanced students supplementary readings are suggested at the end of each chapter.

I am indebted to John Giebink and Frank Farley for their careful reading of the earlier manuscripts and resulting suggestions. Special thanks are also due Steve Owen and Charlene Vogan for their critical reading and useful recommendations in the final stage of manuscript preparation. I am grateful to my wife, Betty, for many editorial comments. Mary J. Gander, of the University of Wisconsin at LaCrosse, not only drew the illustrations but was an excellent critic and source of suggestions.

T. A. RINGNESS

# CONTENTS

## PART TWO
### Affective Behavior from a Behavioral Point of View          39

## Chapter 3

## Chapter 4

# The
# Affective
# Domain
# in Education

## PART ONE

# The Nature and Importance of Affective Learning

In chapters 1 and 2 we shall attempt to define the affective domain and its importance to the individual, society, and to education. As you will see, controversial issues arise, and much research has yet to be done.

The problem is not that affective learning has been neglected as a subject for research in educational psychology or in philosophy and curriculum; but that this is a highly complicated area, and our successes to date have not been impressive. Yet it is increasingly imperative that we pay more attention to this domain. In Part 1 we will learn why.

# Chapter 1

# THE IMPORTANCE
# OF AFFECTIVE LEARNING

Probably the first chapter of a book ought to define the topic of discussion, indicate the importance of the topic, and provide a frame of reference for the reader. This is a large order. It is especially large for this book for two reasons: the topic is ambiguous and controversial, and almost everyone has already chosen sides.

This does not mean, however, that order cannot be brought out of chaos and that various positions cannot be examined. Therefore the topic will be briefly stated; an argument will be made for the relevance of studying it; and some issues and points of view will be presented.

## The Affective Domain as a Topic of Interest

Affective learning deals with the emotional aspects of one's behavior—the influences on our choice of goals, and the means we choose for attaining them. Those aspects include our emotions themselves; our tastes and preferences, attitudes and values, morals and character; and our philosophies of life, or guiding principles.

Although we are aware of affect, few of us consciously realize the extent to which it actually enters our lives. But consider the following illustration:

Tommy is in seventh grade. He is discussing with his parents the events of his day at school.

"It started out *kind of bad* because we had a test — an IQ test. Those always *scare* me and I choke up on them and *don't do well*. And there is always that Pete Smith in class who I *don't like* because he picks on Johnny, and Johnny is one of my *favorite friends*. Pete *looks down on* black people, and never loses a chance to catch Johnny in a mistake, and then he makes a *snide* remark.

"But after the test, things *went better*. We had a real *yummy* lunch, chili-burgers, and in English class we could read about *whatever we wanted*. So I read about beach buggies, and reported orally what I had read. The class *liked* my report, so I'm going to do more of them.

"Then, in social studies, we discussed the Vietnamese people. I think they really *don't care* what sort of government they have, so long as they have *peace*, and *enough to live on*. I think I *agree* with them. Really, most of us *value peace* more than anything else.

"We also got to talking about the *honesty* of some of our politicians, and the *accuracy* of the reporting in the papers and TV. I *feel* that you are either *honest* or not. You can't be *honest* in one situation and not in another, so when I find somebody *dishonest* in one thing, I *can never trust* him again.

"Say, what do you suppose is the matter with Sally? She never raises her hand in class, and when the teacher does call on her, she sometimes *cries*."

As you see, it is not simply what we think, but how we feel about it, that governs our lives.

Only recently has this aspect of learning begun to receive much attention in the schools, although many people are now expressing considerable interest. It has always interested both research and clinical psychologists.

Human behavior is complex, hence difficult to study in its entirety. Accordingly, psychologists and others have found it useful to talk about *domains* of behavior; the usual domains considered are the cognitive, psychomotor, and affective. Although it should be kept in mind that no behavior is entirely cognitive or psychomotor or affective, but has some aspects of each, one may study the more dominant aspects of any act. Such a breakdown can simplify the description of behavior and facilitate its analysis.

The cognitive domain includes all forms of "intellectual" activity — attending, perceiving, remembering, associating, discriminating, analyzing, synthesizing, evaluating — all behaviors that can loosely be called thinking. Activities such as learning to read, to use correct grammar, to remember chemical formulas, or to solve mathematical problems are largely cognitive, and they are very important.

To help teachers and others formulate cognitive teaching objectives, Bloom et al. (1956) developed the classic *Taxonomy of Educa-*

*tional Objectives: Handbook I, The Cognitive Domain.* This taxonomy not only mapped the domain, but showed teachers how to develop learning objectives at each taxonomic level and how to evaluate pupil attainment. The success of this effort led to attempts to develop similar taxonomies in the other two domains.

The psychomotor domain includes all behaviors involving body movements or muscular control. School subjects such as musical performance, athletics and sports, certain vocational arts, handwriting and typewriting, and dance are largely concerned with psychomotor learning. Much is known about this domain, but no comparable taxonomy has been presented, although Simpson, Jewett, and Merrill have developed less extensive taxonomies (Merrill, 1972).

The affective domain includes all behavior connected with feelings and emotions. Thus, as was earlier stated, emotions, tastes and preferences, appreciations, attitudes and values, morals and character, and aspects of personality adjustment or mental health are included.

One finds affective behavior in any school situation — indeed, in *any* situation — but compared to cognitive learning, relatively little affective learning has been deliberately introduced into the curriculum. True, interests and appreciations are fostered in classes in art, music, literature, drama, and dance. Social studies and English classes may deal with motivations, attitudes and values, and sometimes social norms. But comparatively speaking, most teachers do not extensively plan for affective learning experiences.* In addition to the problems mentioned in the Preface, this may in part reflect the belief of many people in our society that the schools should teach "reading, writing, and arithmetic" and stay out of such areas as attitudes and values. Some people hold that the aspects of affective behavior are in the province of the family and the church.

An early attempt to do something about this situation was the development of the *Taxonomy of Educational Objectives: Handbook II, The Affective Domain,* by Krathwohl et al. (1964). The authors discuss interests, appreciations, values, and adjustment, and describe behaviors from simple receiving or awareness of an idea through responding, valuing, organizing, and characterizing. We shall consider this taxonomy more in the next chapter, at which point the relationships of the cognitive and affective domains will be more fully discussed. Many teachers have found the *Taxonomy* useful, although some criticize the approach as being somewhat too directive, or even behavioristically oriented. It should be noted that this taxonomy does not consider the learning of emotional reactions per se, but deals with the rest of the affective domain. As in the cognitive handbook, teachers are aided in stating objectives and evaluating outcomes.

We have to this point differentiated the domains and briefly mentioned how schools may take them into consideration. But not all learning, even in school settings, is planned. Incidental or concomitant learnings may be as important as or even more important than formal learning, and may vitally affect the success of the planned curriculum. For example, in the cognitive domain, the pupil may learn a great deal about the subject at hand without the direction of the teacher, to say nothing of the many skills and the knowledge he gains in unrelated areas. Even more important may be the incidental affective learning that takes place. For example, pupils may learn to feel anxious about tests or marking practices, to become frustrated about disciplinary measures, or to feel inferior because they receive little praise, but much criticism. Additionally, many pupils feel the stress of peer attitudes towards themselves and of racial or sexual discrimination. They may be frustrated because work is too easy or too difficult, or because past or present IQ test performance has caused them to be placed in "ability groups" from which they may never escape. Some teachers, too, because of their personalities and needs, produce negative feelings in students. Thus there are teachers with hostilities, in-

---

* Earlier, of course, were the New England Primer and the McGuffey's readers (which are still used today). Both of these introduce attitudes, values, morals, and character.

securities, unmet affectional needs, or even fears of their own abilities to deal with their pupils, who unwittingly produce all sorts of tension and negative emotion in their pupils (see Ringness, 1968, for further documentation).

On the other hand, of course, many teachers really do consider the effect of their teaching practices upon the pupils' self-esteem and feelings of security and try to foster desirable social interaction among pupils.

## A Look at Means and Ends

The next few paragraphs are preparatory to a distinction which will be made concerning the nature of "education."

What did you do today? Why did you do those things? Why did you do them in the ways you did?

One can give pat answers to these questions, of course, but we can also use them to probe our conceptions of human nature, and of the ways it may be studied. In turn, they lead us to consider appropriate goals in teaching and the best ways to deal with affective learning.

Let us hypothesize that you are now in an early morning class. You awoke, perhaps had a shower, breakfasted, grabbed your materials, and set forth to your classes.

Why? What has caused this series of both simple and complex behaviors to take place? Why not skip breakfast? Why not omit your class and study in the library instead? Why not stay in bed and call in sick?

Decisions may be carefully thought through, or they may be routine, or even so habitual that there do not seem to be reasons at all, as sometimes happens when the comic strip character Dagwood rushes to the office, forgetting that it is Sunday. But in any event, our choices of behavior must rest upon two considerations: the *ends* we wish to attain, and the *means* we have for attaining those ends. Each occurs in an order of precedence, due to many factors including heredity, learning, and the immediate environment. You will recognize the role of one's emotions, attitudes, and values in such determinations. Indeed, Izard et al. (1965) consider affect to be the prime motivational system.

*Means* refers to the possibilities in choices of behavior. What we *can* do, given some goal, depends upon the latitude of choice. We are provided a range of choice by our physical state, our abilities, and the possibilities within the environment. For example, you need not drive a car from home to campus; you can take a bus, ride a bike, or walk. *Means form a locus for choices.*

*Ends* are what we wish to attain. Sometimes they are specific goals and sometimes general. In any instance, some ends produce more powerful effects on our choices than do others. Sometimes we choose a given behavior because we can then attain several ends at once. For

example, one may choose to play football rather than to watch the game because he can gain skill and muscular development, make friendships, develop high morale, and perhaps even attain prestige.

Since any decision-making process must take into account both means and ends, one is freer if he has as many means as possible and if he is clear about the hierarchy of ends he wishes to gain. It is the maximizing of means and the clarification of ends to which the schools must address themselves.*

## Training versus Education

Where do means and ends come from? Let us begin with a rather tenuous distinction between "training" and "education."

### TRAINING

Although not all will agree with our definition, we believe that "training" refers to the activities used by parents, teachers, and others to produce thinking and behavior common to all — conformity. Such behaviors are largely prescribed and directed by the authority figure, reinforced, and otherwise externally controlled.

In the cognitive domain we are trained in common grammatical usage, correct spelling of words, mathematical computations, reading, handwriting, and the speaking of foreign languages, to mention only a few disciplines. The aim is to produce "correct" behaviors.

In the affective domain, society's value system is portrayed by the administration and teachers and by the curriculum. Their attitudes — "this will be good for you," "you should study hard and learn this," "you must not cheat on tests" — are sometimes explicit, but are often implicit in the classroom.

It seems clear that both our means and our ends may be changed by training. What we seek and how we seek it are partly functions of the training processes we undergo.† Training is essentially imposed. It is fostered by the controlling figures in the child's life. In the schools the teacher uses such methods as drill, demonstrations, and lectures. He demands conformity to classroom rules. He evaluates what is

---

* Sometimes means and ends become the same; in other words, means can become ends (e.g., civil rights).
† Lillian Groffman (1971) feels that schools do not meet pupils' needs because of a lack of awareness of changing values. We live in a multifaceted society with divergent values. Pupils can be involved as agents of change. She feels that this may be accomplished by a revelant, humanistic, accepting, and personal approach.

learned and assigns marks accordingly. Much of the teacher's behavior consists of directing that of the pupils.

This is not all bad. It sounds worse than it is, in many instances. After all, many of our needs are satisfied only because society exists, and society can exist only when most of us conform to certain mores. It cannot be "every man for himself"; some training is needed. The main problem is to find the kinds and extent of training needed for us to coexist. (For further clarification of this point you may want to read B. F. Skinner's *Walden Two*.)

Nevertheless, as defined above, training refers to meeting the demands of others and conforming to certain rules and regulations. External control and decision-making are used until the training has been accomplished. The child has few choices: he can accept the training or he can rebel. The latter choice usually produces dire consequences for him, and sometimes for society.

### EDUCATION

"Education" demands inner direction and controls. It implies that a person makes his own decisions, thinks for himself, considers alternatives, and projects the probable consequences of his choices of behavior. He prizes his individualism and accepts responsibility for his own decisions. He relates his means and ends to his own philosophy of life — his hierarchy of values.

Education implies a progression from activities directed by others to self-direction and acceptance of one's unique characteristics. It implies learning to develop one's own talents, to become self-actualizing, and to be aware of the conflicts among one's values and within society. To do this, one must know himself as a person and view himself as acting rather than reacting to his social and physical environment. Further, prizing his own individuality, the educated person must also prize the individuality of others.

Education does not mean simply internalizing attitudes and values learned through training. It also includes a rethinking of these concepts and acceptance of certain ways of living through one's own considered choice. Obviously consideration of affective learning is essential to education; one's tastes and preferences, attitudes and values, ideals and character must be scrutinized and their implications derived, and choices of ends must be made. It is not enough to have learned means (or tools); one must have wisely considered ends.

## The Neglect and Misuse of Affective Learning

Has education been neglected in favor of training? Or have we, in the schools, produced inappropriate affective learning? Quite possibly we have done both in many instances.

The scandals brought to light in pursuing the Watergate affair are an example. Many of the highly placed men brought before the Watergate investigation committee were highly trained in law — yet their ethical commitments seemed strange to a large proportion of the American public.

Again, the "knowledge explosion," coupled with a presumed need to keep America abreast of technological developments such as the Sputnik invented by Russia, has caused pressure on pupils to master vast content areas and to prepare for college, although that trend is now decreasing somewhat. Yet today many students argue that their lives lack meaning. They feel lost in the shuffle, and manipulated. They feel they have not been treated as individuals and have not been seen as persons with the right to decide what and how they will learn. They feel that attempts have been made to indoctrinate them with the "materialistic values of society" and that they have not been given opportunities to look at needed changes in society or ways to institute such changes. In a word, their personal ends have not been properly considered; where ends have been dealt with, they have been the

traditional ends of a traditional society — which means to many students a continuation of manifold evils.

Although the campus scene is not as violently active as it was a few years ago, and although some people feel that students are becoming more conservative, it is still possible to find wild hairdos, odd clothing, pot-smoking, communes, crash pads for runaway teenagers, and many other activities which do not conform to the student stereotype of twenty years ago.

Such behaviors seem to be ways for young people to adjust to the pressures of today's rapidly changing world. Some are trying to form deeper, more meaningful relationships, to be free to be individuals and to accent their individuality; for some disillusioned souls, these behaviors are ways of "copping out."

Some of the activities seem to be symbolic returns to the carefree days of childhood or to incorporate some of the trappings of earlier societies, where population pressures, ecology, inflation, pollution, and the energy crisis had not yet intruded. Mutual support or relatedness are seen as ways to search for values to which one can commit himself, a search for ways to make order out of confusion, to deal with guilt, conflict, and a feeling of impotency, as well as ways to enhance or extend oneself and gain a deeper feeling of the meaning of life. Some students are actively seeking "survival training."

Our students are highly aware of the problems in our society and in the rest of the world. Many of them intend to improve things by obtaining suitable jobs and working within the system. To that end they are studying hard and are seeking new ideas and techniques. They are highly critical of courses that are outdated, hypocritical, irrelevant, or pap. These students seek out members of other cultural groups and try to understand their points of view. Many volunteer to work with handicapped people or the impoverished. And many are highly critical of the "impersonal nature of the university."

Thus homes, early schooling, and the colleges and universities have not provided what many young people are seeking.

Although the schools are certainly not all bad, and although many well-meaning people are attempting to improve the curriculum and school practices, it is still possible to criticize the schools for neglect of affective learning and for failure to provide a more humanistic education. Affective objectives are not clearly stated, and where attitudes have been fostered, alternatives have not been explored. Controversial issues have been skirted or presented in one-sided ways. The differences between minority cultures and middle-class white culture have not been truly examined; rather, the WASP culture has been held up as an ideal to which all should aspire. Little has been

done to enable the student to explore himself. He has been given little assistance in self-direction, gaining independence, and living with his decisions.

Further, the schools have not really concerned themselves with the rub-off of what is taught and the ways it is taught on the emotions, attitudes, and values of students. The well-known work of Holt (1964) is only one of many studies attesting to our failure to adequately consider affective behavior. Holt feels that more often than not, children live in anxiety. Their classroom efforts are more defensive than constructive, and their learning efficiency is consequently hampered. Ringness (1968) has shown that the incidental learning going on in many schools as a result of grading, grouping, disciplinary, and other stress-producing practices contributes to emotional and social maladjustment. It is quite clear that the bright child of middle or higher socioeconomic status who is willing to conform to the teacher's demands will fare best in our schools, but even he would appear to be trained rather than educated.

## Two Points of View

So that you may more clearly understand the organization of this book, we shall briefly discuss two contrasting psychological and philosophical points of view. Neither point of view will be pushed upon you, for no one theory of personality, of learning, or of education is complete and adequate. It therefore becomes necessary to consider various aspects of the human being and his behavior.

Two prominent positions today may be loosely termed "behavioristic" and "humanistic." Because each has been pressed to an extreme, these views *seem* quite antagonistic. Each finds prominent supporters in psychological circles, and each provides a background for educational theory. Each has much to say, but it seems prudent not to push either too far.

The behaviorist views people differently from a humanist. The differences center primarily on the locus of control of behavior, an essential point in regard to the nature of personality.

### THE BEHAVIORISTIC POSITION

A behaviorist emphasizes the environment. Each person is seen as the product of his genes and the learning he gains from his experiences. His attitudes and values, goals and motives, ideas and behaviors, can be traced to genetic, biological, and learned phenomena.

In a sense, each of us is predetermined. We react to our inner and outer environment. The choices we make are the result of that peculiar combination of knowledge, attitudes, and motives which we have accumulated and of the present environmental situation. One might even conclude that we therefore have no real choice of behavior at all.

Each of us is still an individual, due to the vast potential for genetic and experiential differences. But we are not really independent or self-directing; we only think we are. (This is not as pessimistic as it sounds, for most of us do go on with our lives without wondering every minute what is controlling our actions.)

## THE HUMANISTIC POSITION

The behavioristic position does not satisfy many of us. We like to think that we are more than a combination of biological mechanisms and a bundle of learned drives and habits.

Accordingly, it is not surprising that (particularly of late) there has been a strong swing to a humanistic point of view. The humanist states that the controls upon our lives are not nearly as stringent as behaviorists would have us believe. He believes that we can be spontaneous and self-directing, and that we can change if we are not satisfied with the way we are. People are viewed as self-determining and capable of acting rather than simply reacting. They can control their environment rather than letting it control them. Each interacts with others, hence is influenced; but at the same time each influences others. Each person is morally responsible for what he becomes.

The humanist does not deny the influences of genetic endowment or of learning. He argues, however, that there is more to each of us than this; the "whole is more than the sum of its parts." We are seen as complex and self-directed; although we have some difficulty in formulating what makes us self-directing, the humanist believes that it is important for us to learn who we are and to be allowed to be ourselves.

## OTHER DIFFERENCES BETWEEN BEHAVIORISM
## AND HUMANISM

Differences between humanism and behaviorism are not confined to locus of control alone, although that is a central concern. Another important difference concerns the basic human nature. Thus to the behaviorist, a person is neither good nor bad, but essentially a *tabula rasa*. "Good" and "bad" are value judgments; they are made by the society in which we live, and will vary as the society varies. Our behaviors are simply responses to environmental stimuli for which we have been reinforced. The humanist, in contrast, conceives of each person as basically moral and good. If one is not hindered by his environment, he will develop into a moral creature. We need to stimulate him, sometimes, to develop; but primarily we allow him to develop in his own individual way.

Another difference is in regard to the nature of motivation. The behaviorist sees motivation arising primarily from a desire to escape or avoid the unpleasant consequences of behavior and to attain pleasant consequences. We are motivated, of course, to obtain food and satisfy thirst and the like, but much of our motivation to do work is the expectation of reward. Humanists would argue that our main drive is to self-actualize; we desire to develop our own individualities as fully as possible and to be as free from environmental control as possible. (See Chapter 7 for a more detailed discussion of self-actualization.)

Some of the important differences between behaviorism and humanism are seen in Table 1–1. They will become clearer to you as you read on in this book. Part 2 presents a behavioral approach, Part 3 a humanistic approach. But it should be possible to be eclectic in taking a position. Since neither theory is completely satisfactory in explaining personality and behavior, for the present the best we can do is to take whatever seems useful from each theory and use it to best advantage. On the practical level we do see behavior governed

Table 1–1.   *Characteristic Differences Between Behaviorism and Humanism*

|  | Behaviorism | Humanism |
| --- | --- | --- |
| Locus of control | Largely environmental | Largely inner |
| Motivation | Reinforcement | Self-actualization |
| Learning | Governs behavior | Provides locus for choices |
| Attitudes, values | Learned | Considered and compared before adoption |
| Central nature | Neither good nor bad | Good |
| Active, reactive | Largely reactive | Largely active |
| Dependency upon environment | Environmentalist | Inner-directed |
| Freedom | Deterministic | Capable of self-change |

by reinforcement, but we also see spontaneity and independence. The same can be said for any of the items in Table 1–1. Each of us probably reflects both positions; we may perhaps be governed more by our environment and our physical capabilities as children, but we become more self-determining as we mature.

## The Role of the School

The traditional school has tended to emphasize training, conformity, and authority. Values have been preached, and certain behaviors have been promoted. In reaction, many people have turned to "free schools," in which the student determines what he will learn and how he will study it and in which he will develop his own mores and values. Such schools hope to help the student to develop as a person rather than as a product of imposed and socially promoted curricula.

But we are an impulsive and faddist nation. We tend to be extremists. Thus many humanistic ideas have been picked up and played with without adequate attention to possible pitfalls. Further, in experimenting, we have thrown out some of the potentially good things of traditional education. Thus we find "freed-up" schools in which children are confused, lacking in self-discipline, and unable to complete tasks. We find that some children in these schools lack consistent value systems. Sometimes we find "cop-outs," "spoiled brats," and others who suffer from too little direction, which may be as evil as too much. Even Kozol (1972), who is angry with contemporary schools, agrees that free schools have problems; among them is a failure to teach, especially to teach reading.

Powell (1972), an associate justice of the U.S. Supreme Court, says that values imparted to us by others (parents, teachers, neighbors, ministers, and employers) are not always bad. He feels that from others we gain inner strength and conviction, a sense of belonging and of responsibility to others. Many "old values" are still viable: a sense of honor is necessary to self-respect; duty is as important as rights; loyalty, self-discipline, and work are important. What Powell sees is the desire of everyone to "do his own thing," which is anchored in self-interest. As a result we have developed an excessive tolerance of others' behavior, which does not help them in the long run, nor benefit the society that protects and supports them. Powell mentions, as an example, the fact that one university had to withhold grades from over 600 students suspected of purchasing term papers from commercial sources.

Thus, the schools might well need to be more humanistic and to promote individual self-knowledge, the search for meaning and independence, and respect for individual differences. But this does not mean abdicating our roles as teachers. Children do not automatically develop into worthwhile adults. They can become confused, frightened, and hostile if confronted with choices they cannot make because of lack of knowledge, experience, or organized attitudes and values. We also must realize that our own freedoms must end when they interfere with the rights of others.

SUGGESTIONS FOR FURTHER READING

Bereiter, Carl. *Must We Educate?* Englewood Cliffs, N.J.: Prentice-Hall, 1973.
Dember, W. N. "Motivation and the Cognitive Revolution," *American Psychologist*, 29 (1974), 161–68.
Hitt, W. D. "Two Models of Man," *American Psychologist*, 24 (1969), 651–58.
Patterson, C. H. *Humanistic Education*. Englewood Cliffs, N.J.: Prentice-Hall, 1973.
Skinner, B. F. *Walden Two*. New York: Macmillan, 1948.

# Chapter 2

# SOME APPROACHES
# TO THE AFFECTIVE DOMAIN

*Current efforts to define a new kind of education go largely under the name of open education, heralded as "How the schools should be changed" by Silberman(1970). As Silberman notes, much of the ideology of open education rests upon the thought of Piaget, and is in that sense the same developmental ideology that lay behind Dewey's progressive education. However, unlike Dewey's approach, open education whether in the United States or Britain has not clearly defined its positive ends. When it does so, it will probably follow Dewey in defining education as the stimulation of universal lines of human development. Such definitions can only be made empirical by longitudinal studies of the effects of educational experience as these relate first to the natural lines of human development and second to a reflective or philosophic appraisal of the meaning and worth of the various lines of development. Such an undertaking is a new, large, lengthy and difficult task for educational psychology. Can it settle for less?*

— LAWRENCE KOHLBERG

## The Taxonomic Approach

Strictly speaking, any behavior that has an emotional tone lies within the affective domain, which is why emotions themselves belong to it. Some behaviors have a more highly cognitive component than emotions per se, yet also have a definite emotional tone. Thus, interests, tastes, preferences, attitudes, values, morals, character, and personality adjustment are important parts of the affective domain.

Krathwohl et al. (1964) concern themselves with all aspects of the affective domain except emotions and personality adjustment. They have developed the *Taxonomy of Educational Objectives, Handbook II: The Affective Domain* to classify various affective behaviors. The *Taxonomy* portrays a continuum of internalization (see Figure 2–1). Thus in the beginning of one's experience, one can be only peripherally involved with a particular object or idea; that is, one can be aware of the existence of that object or idea. Further along the taxonomy it is possible to become more deeply involved, as in responding to the object or idea, developing positive feelings for it, or even making it a whole way of life.

The *Taxonomy* is neutral. Although the terminology is positive, it applies equally well to negative attitudes and values. For example, a person might be placed on the continuum anywhere from awareness, responding, and so on, through valuing racism or even being characterized by it. In a word, either "positive" or "negative" affect fits into the taxonomic structure; and, indeed, what some persons consider positive might be regarded as negative by others — for example, my steadfastness is your stubbornness.

Figure 2–1 shows the entire continuum of receiving, responding, valuing, organizing, and characterizing by a value complex. It also shows the dimensions encompassed by interests, appreciations, attitudes, values, and personal adjustment. It is clear that each aspect of affective behavior encompasses several dimensions of the continuum; it may not be quite so clear that the divisions between receiving and responding, for example, are not hard and fast, but somewhat vague. Thus it is difficult to distinguish between one who has an "attitude" and one who has a "value," although those concepts are useful for the teacher.

To illustrate, let us presume that a teacher is anxious to deal with the "problem of pollution." At first the students may simply become aware of the words and the concepts; at that point they are neither for nor against pollution. As they become interested, they become willing to listen to discussion and to read material on the topic. Still later, they may even read about pollution to the exclusion of other choices they may be offered. So far, however, they will not have taken a position.

The second stage, responding, requires the students to form an opinion. They may at first simply go along with the teacher's position—that is, acquiesce. They have not actually chosen the position as a matter of internal conviction. Later a student might show that he

Figure 2–1.  Range of Meaning of Commonly Used Affective Terms Measured Against the Taxonomy Continuum

| Taxonomy Continuum | | Affective Terms (ranges) | | | | |
|---|---|---|---|---|---|---|
| 1.0 RECEIVING | 1.1 Awareness | | | | | INTEREST |
| | 1.2 Willingness to Receive | | | | | |
| | 1.3 Controlled or Selected Attention | | | | | |
| 2.0 RESPONDING | 2.1 Acquiescence in Responding | | | | APPRECIATION | INTEREST |
| | 2.2 Willingness to Respond | ADJUSTMENT | VALUE | ATTITUDES | | |
| | 2.3 Satisfaction in Response | | | | | |
| 3.0 VALUING | 3.1 Acceptance of a Value | | | | | |
| | 3.2 Preference for a Value | | | | | |
| | 3.3 Commitment | | | | | |
| 4.0 ORGANIZATION | 4.1 Conceptualization of a Value | | | | | |
| | 4.2 Organization of a Value System | | | | | |
| 5.0 CHARACTERIZATION BY A VALUE COMPLEX | 5.1 Generalized Set | | | | | |
| | 5.2 Characterization | | | | | |

is beginning to take a position against pollution by willingly stating his feelings in public. Still later he shows that he is quite convinced of his position, and defends it when necessary.

At the third level, the student has broadened his base of thinking and has internalized his position even more. He now accepts the need for managing the environment, incorporates his position into his hierarchy of values, and becomes committed. Here he has internalized his point of view; his own beliefs, rather than the opinions of others, will govern his actions.

Later such a student may organize his views on the managed environment into his total value system, along with his views on such issues as population control and civil rights. And eventually he may generalize even more, becoming involved in a career in the field, or otherwise characterizing his whole way of life by such issues.

The *Taxonomy* provides illustrative teaching objectives and test items for evaluating learning outcomes. (There is also an extensive statement of the theoretical orientation from which the taxonomy was developed.)

## Klausmeier's Position

Herbert Klausmeier and Richard Ripple (1971) use somewhat different dimensions in conceptualizing the affective domain. For them, stability, scope, subjectivity, significance to self, and significance to society are important.

Thus tastes or preferences are temporary. Your taste in literature, food, or music has probably changed throughout your life. Your tastes are specific to the object: "I like ripe olives; I don't like Bach." They are not highly internalized and are more a function of the object itself than of any internal conviction. They are not highly significant to the self — it really makes little difference whether you prefer green or red shirts or socks. Finally, except for manufacturers or salespeople, society is not too concerned whether you prefer a Thunderbird or a Riviera. (But perhaps in view of the energy crisis, that last statement should be questioned!)

An attitude is a step further to generalization, internalization, centrality to self, and significance to self and society. As Klausmeier defines them, attitudes are emotionally toned predispositions to react in a consistent way, favorably or unfavorably, toward a person, object, or idea. They contain "feeling tone," sometimes quite irrational, which influences the acceptance or rejection of the object or the attitude. They also contain a cognitive aspect, in which one has internalized his views toward the object, and an action aspect, in which one seems predisposed to a particular overt behavior toward the object. For example, one may have an attitude against racism. He emotionally rejects racism in himself and others, defends his feelings, and will do all in his power to counteract such racism.

Attitudes are directional rather than neutral and prepare one to be motivated in certain ways. They are more stable than tastes or preferences. For example, one may feel favorably or unfavorably about "education," and that attitude tends to continue over time. It is more general than a taste in that it encompasses many activities that can be blanketed under the term "education"; it is more deeply internalized and conceptualized, and more subjective. Its significance to the self is greater, since it involves one's feelings about how he was educated, as well as what steps he might take for further education. And it is of higher significance to society, since the combined attitudes of many people determine the nature and scope of public education.

Values are even more deeply internalized, and affect entire ways of life. They help to determine what one considers moral or immoral and thus contribute to what is often called character. For example, one might value "freedom of thought." To this end he would resent and combat any attempts to indoctrinate himself or others. He would prize freedom of the press, of religion, and of politics. Such values may permeate an entire society. Furthermore, if one values freedom of thought in the abstract, he must value it for others as well as for himself. Thus a person with this value would be open to other persons' points of view. He would be inquiring and would welcome differing opinions.

One's value system may be so pervasive that he builds his life around it; to do this, he must have either a cohesive, integrated value system or a highly dominant single value. This is really what is meant by the term "character." Thus the character of Christ might be said to be that of compassion; that of Caesar, conquest.

## Some Relationships Between the Cognitive and Affective Domains

It is probably obvious that attitudes and values have a cognitive as well as an affective component. That is, they are not simply composed of feelings for or against something, but include intellectualization as well. For example, one may value "human rights"; he has both a feeling tone which may cause him to become quite passionate when he feels someone's rights have been violated (for example, by rioting crowds or by official bombing) and a cognitive ability to verbalize his values, to defend them logically, and to state how he arrived at them.

Krathwohl et al. (1964) make a good case for parallelism between the earlier taxonomy of the cognitive domain (Bloom et al., 1956) and the affective taxonomy. We will center upon two of their points: the use of cognitive objectives as means to affective goals and the use of affective objectives as means to cognitive goals. You may wish to explore them further on your own.

### COGNITIVE OBJECTIVES AS MEANS
### TO AFFECTIVE GOALS

As we will see further in a later chapter, schools frequently indoctrinate students with certain points of view. For example, Krathwohl says, we want our students to learn to recognize "good" poetry, music, etc. Teachers are less likely to want to indoctrinate in many aspects of "moral" education and will wish to avoid dealing with religion in the public schools, but they frequently bring up opposing points of view for class discussion, and they sometimes ask pupils to play roles, debate, participate in panel discussions, and the like.

In effect, we can use cognitive means to bring about affective learning, since learning *about* something, such as the Black Experience, can produce attitudinal change.

### AFFECTIVE OBJECTIVES AS MEANS
### TO COGNITIVE GOALS

Krathwohl says that we can try to contribute to positive affect in the student in order to motivate his cognitive learning. This is another way of saying that we may try to create interest, curiosity, a feeling of pleasure when material is mastered, and enjoyment of the learning tasks themselves. We may try to get the child to internalize the values of learning and achievement, of being industrious, and so on.

On the other hand, we may use the threat of poor marks, failure, or other negative means to try to motivate him, although such tactics are not wise or effective. Similarly, we may try to attain classroom discipline and knowledge of the rules and laws of the school by posing threats or punishment.

### SIMULTANEOUS ATTAINMENT OF COGNITIVE
### AND AFFECTIVE GOALS

One can, of course, attempt both cognitive and affective learning simultaneously, although such learning may be difficult. One problem, according to Krathwohl, is that "one domain tends to drive out the other." That is, emphasis upon interests, attitudes, and values, and on forming one's own opinions, may result in the extreme in the kind of class where there are no correct answers and each person's ideas are as good as any other person's, and where argument or discussion takes precedence over attainment of knowledge. Equally possible, of course, are classes that are so highly cognitive or intellectual that they are sterile affectively.

It should be clear that only a highly skilled teacher who has many techniques and is clear about his objectives can produce both cognitive and affective learning without doing violence to one or the other. Most teachers, unfortunately, begin with both objectives, but (as stated in the Preface) the affective domain usually loses out. Perhaps your consideration of the ideas of this book may change that situation in your own teaching.

We now come to two issues which require some clarification. Following this, we can delineate some particular concerns of the school.

## Two Important Issues

### THE DESIRABILITY OF TEACHING
### ATTITUDES AND VALUES

Should the school engage in teaching or stimulating various attitudes and values? If we say "yes," we then have to agree on which attitudes and values to promote. For example, Klausmeier and Goodwin (1966) have suggested that the following attitudes are worth fostering:

Liking for the subject being presented
Liking for teachers
Liking for classmates
Liking for school generally
Starting work promptly
Working with enthusiasm and vigor
Following directions
Taking care of property
Observing safety rules
Being courteous to others

Some students have said that the attitudes in this list smack of conformity. But few disagreed with the idea of fostering self-respect in pupils, respect for others, openmindedness, freedom from prejudice, and the promotion of individuality and self-actualization.

We might agree to explore various attitudes and values and allow pupils to come to their own conclusions. One approach to this is the value clarification approach of Raths et al. (1966), which will be discussed further in Chapter 8.

We frequently hear that the schools tend to foster WASP values, or middle-class values, and that this is detrimental to black children or those at lower socioeconomic levels whose values are different. We also hear that schools should begin to study minority group values and to appreciate their worth, incorporating many of them into the white or middle-class society. Since our country is a cultural plurality, various subcultures and accompanying values should be allowed to coexist.

We are also aware that many people question traditional attitudes and behaviors, feeling that society needs change. Accordingly, schools might well explore as many positions as possible on various issues and help children to project the consequences of the positions they might take and come to their own conclusions.

Or we might decide that the schools should stay out of the affective domain. It can be argued that the schools have no business dealing with moral development, that that aspect of life should be left to parents, the ministry, and the law. This position makes it mandatory for the schools to deal with cognitive knowledge and skills only and to keep hands off the personalities of the children. Carl Bereiter (1973) is one writer who believes that schools should not try to change children, but simply enlarge their realm of choice by providing basic tools.

All of this leaves the teacher in somewhat of a bind. In the first place, simply by being a person, he is illustrating a value system. Furthermore, in any society there seem to be at least *some* pervasive values (for example, the Bill of Rights), and as agents of society, the school must adhere to them. For a society to exist there must be *some* communality of values, and if the schools remain aloof from promoting them, other agencies such as the mass media or the peer culture may well preempt the schools' influence. Sometimes these agencies are self-seeking, resulting in such things as the drug culture, disrespect for law, negative attitudes toward the police, and changing sex mores.

Our answer to this problem can only be in coming to grips with the question of *moral relativism* as opposed to *moral absolutism*. J. R. Fraenkel (1969) considers the question at length. The moral relativist argues that different cultures have differing values, and that to each culture, its own values are correct. Thus there are no absolutes, and if someone thinks he is right, his views are as legitimate as those of anyone else. Therefore one should not *teach* a system of values, although he might explore various values with his pupils. In contrast, the moral absolutist believes certain values permeate all societies; since those values are transcendent, they should be taught or stimulated.

Let us turn to some of the work of Lawrence Kohlberg and his associates as a possible solution to our dilemma. Kohlberg (1973) finds difficulty with some so-called cop-outs the schools have employed in dealing with the problem of moral relativity. The first, he says, is to call moral education *socialization*. In learning to conform to the teacher's expectations and the school rules, the child is becoming "socialized"; he is internalizing the norms and standards of society. This approach ignores the fact that not all people believe in the same rules and regulations; many consider that the rules should be changed.

The second cop-out is the "bag of virtues" approach, in which children are expected to learn to be honest, loyal, friendly, and so on. The problem Kohlberg (1973, pp. 4–5) sees in this approach is that

vague consensus on the goodness of these terms conceals a great deal of actual disagreement over their definitions. What is one man's "integrity" is another man's "stubbornness," what is one man's *honesty* in "expressing your true feelings" is another man's *insensitivity* to the feelings of others. This is evidenced in controversial fields of adult behavior. Student protestors view their behavior as reflecting the virtues of altruism, idealism, awareness, courage. Those in opposition regard the same behavior as reflecting the vice of irresponsibility and disrespect for "law and order."

Another approach that is widely acclaimed is the "mental health" approach. In this the child is encouraged to attain such characteristics as self-confidence, spontaneity, curiosity, and self-discipline. The problem here, according to Kohlberg, is that these traits or virtues come from the verbal connotations of their terms rather than from a firm base in psychological findings or philosophic principles. Further, it has not been shown that any of the above lines of endeavor can predictably determine the traits a child will carry into adulthood.

Kohlberg therefore takes a cognitive-developmental view of the nature of moral education (Kohlberg and Turiel, 1971; Kohlberg, 1973), based in part on his own cross-cultural and international study of moral stages and values. As opposed to moral relativism, Kohlberg argues that there are universal values to be found throughout all civilizations.

Kohlberg was influenced by John Dewey and Jean Piaget. As you may be aware, Piaget postulated developmental trends in cognitive behavior; children must pass through the initial (infantile) stage of the sensorimotor period, into the preoperational stage, then the stage

Table 2–1.  *Kohlberg's Moral Stages*

---

I. PRECONVENTIONAL LEVEL

At this level the child is responsive to cultural rules and labels of good and bad, right or wrong, but interprets these labels in terms of either the physical or the hedonistic consequences of the action (punishment, reward, exchange of favors) or in terms of the physical power of those who enunciate the rules and labels. The level is divided into the following two stages:

Stage 1:  *The punishment and obedience orientation.* The physical consequences of action determine its goodness or badness regardless of the human meaning or value of these consequences. Avoidance of punishment and unquestioning deference to power are valued in their own right, not in terms of respect for an underlying moral order supported by punishment and authority (the latter being Stage 4.)

Stage 2:  *The instrumental relativist orientation.* Right action consists of that which instrumentally satisfies one's own needs and occasionally the needs of others. Human relations are viewed in terms like those of the marketplace. Elements of fairness, reciprocity, and equal sharing are present, but they are always interpreted in a physical pragmatic way. Reciprocity is a matter of "you scratch my back and I'll scratch yours," not of loyalty, gratitude, or justice.

II. CONVENTIONAL LEVEL

At this level, maintaining the expectations of the individual's family, group, or nation is perceived as valuable in its own right, regardless of immediate and obvious consequences. The attitude is one not only of *conformity* to personal expectations and social order, but of loyalty to it, of actively *maintaining*, supporting, and justifying the order and of identifying with the persons or group involved in it. At this level, there are the following two stages:

Stage 3:  *The interpersonal concordance or "good boy–nice girl" orientation.* Good behavior is that which pleases or helps others and is approved by them. There is much conformity to stereotypical images of what is majority or "natural" behavior. Behavior is frequently judged by intention — "He means well" becomes important for the first time. One earns approval by being "nice."

Stage 4:  *The "law and order" orientation.* There is orientation toward authority, fixed rules, and the maintenance of the social order. Right behavior consists of doing one's duty, showing respect for authority, and maintaining the given social order for its own sake.

III. POST-CONVENTIONAL, AUTONOMOUS, OR PRINCIPLED LEVEL

At this level, there is a clear effort to define moral values and principles which have validity and application apart from the authority of

Table 2–1. (*Continued*)

---

the groups or persons holding these principles and apart from the individual's own identification with these groups. This level again has two stages:

Stage 5: *The social-contract legalistic orientation generally with utilitarian overtones.* Right action tends to be defined in terms of general individual rights and in terms of standards which have been critically examined and agreed upon by the whole society. There is a clear awareness of the relativism of personal values and opinions and a corresponding emphasis upon procedural rules for reaching consensus. Aside from what is constitutionally and democratically agreed upon, the right is a matter of personal "values" and "opinion." The result is an emphasis upon the "legal point of view," but with an emphasis upon the possibility of changing law in terms of rational considerations of social utility (rather than freezing it in terms of Stage 4, "law and order"). Outside the legal realm, free agreement, and contract is the binding element of obligation. This is the "official" morality of the American government and Constitution.

Stage 6: *The universal ethical principle orientation.* Right is defined by the decision of conscience in accord with self-chosen *ethical principles* appealing to logical comprehensiveness, universality, and consistency. These principles are abstract and ethical (the Golden Rule, the categorical imperative), they are not concrete moral rules like the Ten Commandments. At heart, these are universal principles of *justice*, of the *reciprocity* and *equality* of the human *rights* and or respect for the dignity of human beings as *individual persons*.

---

From Kohlberg, Lawrence, "The Contribution of Developmental Psychology to Education — Examples from Moral Education," *Educational Psychologist*, 10 (1973), 7–8. Copyright © 1973 by APA Division 15. Reprinted with permission.

of concrete operations, and finally the stage of formal operations. These stages tend to follow a fairly consistent time span, with the formal operations stage occurring about the time of adolescence. The stages follow in the same order among all children, and they are not reversible. One cannot teach a higher stage than the child is ready for, but when the child is ready, one can help stimulate him to move to the next higher stage.

Kohlberg believes that a similar series of stages of moral development also exists (see Table 2–1); however, he does not feel that everyone automatically progresses to the highest levels; stimulation of attainment is frequently necessary, and some adults have never moved beyond some of the lower moral stages.

Among the universal highest-order values are "Life, Law, Roles of Affection, Property, Contract and Trust, Liberty, Social Order and Authority, and Equity" (Kohlberg, 1973, p. 6). When we find people holding other values, it may be that they have not attained the highest-order values, or it may be that they are expressing the same values in different ways.

Kohlberg believes that we should stimulate children to move to higher moral stages, arguing that this is constitutional, philosophically justified, and socially useful (Kohlberg and Turiel, 1971). In Chapter 8 we will see how this may be done.

What, then, shall we conclude? There may well be some pervasive values common to most cultures, if indeed they are not universal. There are also lower-order rules, customs, laws, and the like, perhaps confused, perhaps differing from group to group, which must be dealt with on the way to ultimate morality. Our role may then be dual. That is, we might attempt to promote whatever pervasive values we can identify. We might also attempt to stimulate children to move from immature, low-level moral stages to higher-level, more mature stages of moral development. It should be recognized, however, that a position such as this must be tentative, since, as Kohlberg's remarks (quoted at the beginning of this chapter) indicate, we do not yet know enough about the relationship of the educational experience to the natural lines of human development; nor have we attained a common philosophy concerning which lines of development should be encouraged.

## THE EFFECT OF VALUES ON BEHAVIOR

A second issue is whether, having developed a value system, one will overtly act in accordance with it. The reader may remember the newspaper accounts of Kitty Genovese, who was murdered during a period of a full half hour in view of over thirty spectators. None of those spectators intervened in any way or called the police. On the other hand, at least some persons have become sufficiently aware of the need to carry their values into action, as evidenced by the lives of Albert Schweitzer and Mahatma Ghandi.

What factors determine whether one will or will not act upon his values? Psychological literature contains some interesting studies of willingness to carry into action such values as helpfulness to others in distress, and psychologists have found a number of factors specific to the situation. For example, when a person was posed fixing a tire by the roadside, the likelihood of a motorist's stopping depended upon whether the person was a woman or a man, young or old.

In examining reasons why attitudes are not always consistent with observed behaviors, Kelman (1974) points out that although one tends to state attitudes conforming to those prescribed by his reference groups, they may not adequately reflect his own true views. Thus, for example, in regard to racial issues, students may express considerable tolerance, yet in a concrete situation may not be able to act with the same amount of tolerance.

In predicting behavior from attitudes, it is also necessary to separate one's generalized attitude toward a group from his attitude toward a specific person of that group. For example, is your attitude toward Henry Aaron consistent with your attitude toward black people in general? What if we were to substitute the name of Malcolm X?

There is also the question of the degree to which one is committed to a given value. Thus Raths et al. (1966) make the point that a child may not really know clearly how he feels about various issues or what he is striving for. They feel that a clear system of values is necessary if one is to become positive in his approach to others, to be purposeful, to be reasonably proud of himself as a functioning individual, and to be enthusiastic about what he does. Raths further says that when one lacks a clear system of values he is more vulnerable to confusion, hence to insecurity. Resulting behavior patterns may include apathy, overdissension, overconformity, flightiness, drifting, uncertainty and inconsistency, and even role-playing, or wearing a mask.

This is not all. One must come to some conclusion concerning his hierarchy of values. Which ones override which others? Under what circumstances? When we think of Kitty Genovese, we must remember that fear of involvement and reprisal, concern for the safety of one's family and oneself, and other possible values may override the desire to aid someone in distress.

Attitudes and behavior are therefore not always consistent. It follows that schools cannot deal merely on the abstract plane with attitudes and values, but must find ways to present concrete situations, both real and contrived, to help pupils learn how committed they are to their values and how those values can be carried out in overt behavior. This subject, too, will be dealt with in later chapters.

## Some Specific Concerns

We teachers realize that children come to us with an affective structure or background already built in. That is, they already have interests, emotional reactions, likes and dislikes, attitudes and values, and

other affective behavior learned from the home, peer group, street corner, television, and other sources. We must meet them "where they are" and carry on from there.

We have had a general discussion of some of the problems and issues. Let us focus on a few more specific topics.

### THE SELF-CONCEPT

It is clear that the ways one regards himself are influential in determining how he views his life experiences and in turn, how he behaves. The total of one's attitudes about himself is called the self-concept, the function of which is to act as a mediator between one's motives, the stimuli impinging upon him, and his responses to the situation.

For example, if a child is certain that he is stupid, he may not try to learn. If he feels unaccepted by others, he may withdraw. If he feels self-accepting, he may try hard to excel. How he feels about himself affects not only the ways he interacts with others, but the ways he deals with any situation. Children's self-attitudes directly affect their learning in the classroom, their interactions with teachers and peers, and indeed, every aspect of their school lives.

The self-concept is formed cognitively, largely from the feedback one gets from others. It is affective, however, in that one is happy or unhappy with this feedback. One tends to internalize it, and in turn evaluates oneself as adequate or inadequate, acceptable or unacceptable, and so on in other dimensions, each of which has emotional tone. Schools need to promote healthy self-concepts by providing success experiences; equally, they must refrain from damaging children's self-concepts by allowing them to infer that they are inferior, unwanted, or disliked.

The self-concept will be treated in more detail in Chapter 8. Consider here, however, some of these teachers' remarks, heard in a teachers' lounge:

"I just can't bear another Jones kid in my room. All the older ones have been so dirty and stupid."

"You can't expect much from Billy Smith. He's from a deprived home."

"I may have to teach him, but I don't have to like him."

Do you think these feelings can be concealed? What teacher behaviors might result? What effects on the children's self-concept?

MOTIVATION

Motivation initiates, maintains, and controls the extent and direction of behavior. In school, motivation is one of the most important factors in learning, along with intelligence and previous background of learning. Motivation is a factor in discipline, pupil adjustment, and classroom relationships.

The affective domain is highly relevant to motivation, and indeed, one can almost conceive of motivation as another affective dimension, although actually it is broader than that. But it is true that emotions themselves have motivating force; we act to reduce our fears or anxieties and to further joy and affection.

We have already seen that the direction of one's behavior is governed by his attitudes and values, which predispose him to be for or against certain things. Have you ever heard or said things like these?

"I don't see why we have to do this."

"I get sick every time the teacher announces a test."

"I don't know what I want to do, so why should I study?"

"Arithmetic is so picky; I detest it."

What motives are being portrayed? Do they seem to be desirable and healthy? Are there ways we can work to modify them?

### INFORMATION PROCESSING

What one listens to, what he perceives others as saying, and how he reacts to what is said depends upon his emotional state, his attitudes and values, and his personal adjustment. What pupils gain from reading, lectures, or class discussions obviously will vary with their respective affective states. Information consistent with one's value system is easily attended to and assimilated; information at odds with these tends to be shut out, misunderstood, or otherwise negatively processed. Obviously, schools must understand pupils' attitudes and adjust teaching practices accordingly if they are to be relevant and heeded.

### LEARNING

Learning and performance are frequently confused. We infer learning from performance; that is, if one can perform an act, it is reasonable to assume he has learned. On the other hand, if he does not perform an act when requested, we cannot infer that he has not learned it. There may be many reasons for not so performing, among them a refusal to do so.

We are saying that students may know many things they do not use in practice. There are many times when we know what we ought to do but do not do it. For example, we ought to stop smoking, we ought to study our lessons, we ought to save our money — and what else? Thus, although the cognitive domain is important for learning, unless affective learning also takes place, the cognitive aspects may never be used; they may not seem relevant.

### ANXIETY

Holt's position, that children tend to live with anxiety too much of the time, was mentioned earlier. Kaplan (1970) points out that some anxiety is probably normal and even necessary, in order to provide a need for greater competency — that is, to learn. But when it is overwhelming, the child cannot respond constructively.* Teachers need to know the source and degree of anxiety to be able to respond helpfully.

---

* The subject of anxiety is complex; it will be treated in more detail in Chapter 3.

It should be clear that when one is highly anxious, much of his energy is directed to finding ways of reducing that anxiety. In the classroom this may involve finding ways to please the teacher, circumvent the teacher, avoid the classroom or school entirely, get others to take responsibility for one's work, and so on. Defense mechanisms — denying of the reality of such behavior as cheating on tests, blaming others, rationalizing one's inadequate behaviors, or excusing oneself on the basis that everyone else is doing poorly also — are used.

A much studied subject is *test anxiety*. Some students become upset at even the thought of taking a test. They become unable to think efficiently, are confused and tense, and therefore do poorly on the test. Again, almost all of us have also experienced stage fright and noticed the effects on our performance. And most athletes have had the experience of being so anxious about an important game that they muffed the ball, even though they had played well during practice.

Anxiety is an affective state. The schools must become aware of how to reduce pupil anxiety and how to help children to handle it when it does occur.

COMMUNICATION

The teacher tends to set the tone for classroom communication. This is unfortunate in a way, because the teacher often does most of the talking, and soon the children know more about him than he does about them.

We shall consider teacher-pupil communication more later. At this point it is sufficient to point out that classroom communication must be open, honest, and a two-way street. Communication should be positive and enriching for students and teacher. Thus the teacher should wish to accept and encourage affective as well as cognitive expressions from his charges.

Unfortunately, few teachers feel secure enough to tolerate a pupil's expression of boredom, frustration, or anger, and many teachers either authoritatively shut off the pupil's attempt to state how he feels or become defensive and try to justify themselves, implying that the child is at fault. A healthy teacher is realistic and knows that children can have negative as well as positive feelings and that those feelings may well be justified. Such a teacher tries to learn from the honest expressions of the children for the ultimate benefit of both. For example, if a pupil states that he is bored with a discussion, instead of feeling threatened the teacher might pursue the pupil's statement to gain useful information for improving the discussion and gaining rapport with the child. Although it is not easy, if the teacher can share feelings openly with his pupils, he can learn much from them.

### AFFECTIVE LEARNING AND SOCIETY

That our society has troubles need not be pursued at length, for we have been hearing this from all sides for some time. The "problem" is basically to define the problem. Some have said that society lacks clear goals; others have said that the goals for which we are working are untenable. This concern for direction can be noticed in the classroom as well as in the media. It is apparent that exploration of motives, goals, means, ends, attitudes, and values must be our prime curricular concerns. Issues must be openly and honestly discussed rather than skirted or ignored. The teacher as well as the pupils must learn to listen to others, try to understand them, evaluate his own opinions, consider alternatives, and weigh consequences.

Ordinarily, young people are more open and willing to explore and change than older people, always excepting some bigoted extremists who want freedom for themselves but deny it to others. After all, older people resist change because changes are threatening; they may negate a lifetime of activity within a person's attitudinal framework. It is surprising, nevertheless, to see how many older persons really are reexamining their views.

School pupils must also be willing to explore and perhaps to change, yet many are prejudiced or rigid. They may have modelled themselves uncritically after parents or peers without having thought through what they themselves really stand for. The schools must address themselves to this problem. They should be safe places to develop the openness that is required, where pupils can compare their own value systems with those of others and explore the advantages of differing points of view. If they can be encouraged to do this, we can hope for a generation of young adults who will not only tolerate individual differences among people but actually prize them. Such adults will accept innovation, relate well to various cultures, and be more able to deal constructively with the ills of our society.

## A Look Ahead

We have developed the nature and relevance of the affective domain to educators and briefly explored some rather complicated issues. The balance of the book is divided into two parts: the first deals with a behavioristic orientation to the affective domain and the second with a humanistic approach. Many of the points discussed here will be treated in more detail, and new problems and issues will be developed.

## SUGGESTIONS FOR FURTHER READING

Klausmeier, H. J., and Ripple, R. E. *Learning and Human Abilities*, 3rd ed. New York: Harper and Row, 1971, Chapter 14.

Kohlberg, L. "The Contribution of Developmental Psychology to Education — Examples from Moral Education," *Educational Psychologist*, 10 (1973), 2–14.

Kohlberg, L., and Turiel, E. "Moral Development and Moral Education," in Lesser, G. S. (ed), *Psychology and Educational Practice*. Glenview, Ill.: Scott, Foresman, 1971.

Krathwohl, D. R., Bloom, B. S., and Masia, B. B. *Taxonomy of Educational Objectives, Handbook II: The Affective Domain*. New York: David McKay, 1964. Chapters 1–4.

Postman, N., and Weingartner, C. "A Careful Guide to the School Squabble," *Psychology Today*, 7 (1973), 76–86.

Rich, J. M. *Education and Human Values*. Reading, Mass.: Addison-Wesley, 1968.

Ringness, T. A. *Mental Health in the Schools*. New York: Random House, 1968, Chapter 1.

Tomkins, S. S., and Izard, C. E. *Affect, Cognition, and Personality*. New York: Springer, 1965. Chapters 1–3.

## PART TWO

# Affective Behavior
# from a Behavioral Point of View

The next four chapters deal with the affective domain largely from a behavioristic, or "learning theory," point of view. This is a respectable, traditional way of looking at affective behavior, and has the weight of much research behind it. One should not assume, however, that it lacks humaneness; indeed, B. F. Skinner has signed the Humanistic Manifesto II. But behaviorism is different from humanistic psychology.

There are many learning theories, of course. We shall be concerned with classical and operant conditioning, social learning theory (identification and imitation), and cognitive theory. Each has its place and all must be examined, since none can explain all learning or behavior.

As you read the next four chapters, you may be able to relate them to the moral stages Kohlberg talks about, as well as to the *Taxonomy* and to Klausmeier's point of view.

# Chapter 3

# CLASSICAL CONDITIONING
# AND AFFECTIVE BEHAVIOR

Once upon a time a young psychologist wanted to train his small son to the potty. Since children don't ordinarily find the seat too comfortable or stimulating, he decided to change its image by introducing an element of pleasure. He obtained a circus poster of a clown — colorful, smiling, with a big nose. He then placed a red light bulb in the nose and switched it on while the child was on the potty. The child was entranced and often wanted to go to the bathroom. Later, it wasn't difficult to rig an electrical circuit so that when the child urinated, a connection was made, and there was the lighted red nose.

But conditioning processes often produce stimulus generalization, which means that stimuli like the original, specific stimulus can evoke a similar response.

As you might anticipate, father and son went for a car ride one day and were stopped by a big red traffic light. Guess what happened!

But some conditioning isn't funny. Most teachers have experienced one or more of the following:

Four-year-old Mary comes to nursery school with her mother, but when Mother leaves, Mary cries and carries on, with strong emotional behavior. Only when Mother promises to stay does Mary quiet down again. She continues to watch fearfully lest Mother show some signs of abandoning her.

Peter becomes slightly nauseated whenever a test is announced. Sometimes he becomes actively sick and has to go home.

41

And Monday depresses us — that's why it's "Blue Monday." But we enjoy Friday — it is T.G.I.F. (Thank God It's Friday).

If you asked Mary, Peter, or yourself why these feelings occurred, you would probably get an answer, but it might well be a rationalization rather than the truth. That is because we frequently don't know enough about our real reasons for feeling as we do, although we can call upon our intellect for an explanation that may satisfy us. The behaviors described above can be considered examples of *classical conditioning*, in which form of learning we are frequently unaware that we are learning, and are certainly not motivated to try.

Classical conditioning has been studied largely in regard to reflexes, which are biological behaviors. Here, however, we shall primarily consider emotional behavior, since it is so important to the schools.

You may be surprised to learn that emotions themselves are biological; yet they are. Accordingly, we will first spend some time considering the nature of emotions; we then will become acquainted with the nature of classical conditioning; and finally, we will deal with some practical illustrations in the school setting.


## Emotions

It is trite to say that schools should try to cultivate pleasant emotions such as joy, excitement, love and friendship, and pleasure in school tasks, and that anger, hostility, fear, or anxiety should be prevented or alleviated. Not only are we humanitarian, but pleasant emotions are more apt to further the work of the school through positive motivation to attend and learn. Yet experience tells us that although small children are eager and excited about going to school, as they grow older they are more apt to have negative feelings about school and school tasks. We cannot blame the schools entirely for this change, but it is something we cannot ignore.

The term "feelings" is sometimes used to describe the cognitive aspect of emotions — that is, the fact that we "know" we are angry, or that we feel some other emotion. "Emotions," then, refers to the biological aspects of emotional experiences. For our purposes we shall use "emotions" to refer to both aspects.

Emotions are governed by two separate but interacting nervous systems: the central nervous system (CNS) and the autonomic nervous system (ANS). When the sense organs react to an emotionally arousing stimulus, such as the sight of a handsome person or the scent of perfume, a nerve impulse from the sense organ is passed through the lower-order, nonthinking areas of the brain.*

Two reactions occur. One is that the ANS is activated and produces various physiological changes. We become aroused (motivated) in various ways. The other reaction is cognitive; we become intellectually aware of what we are experiencing. The CNS recognizes or labels the emotion as fear, anger, or pleasure, and chooses behavior that will do something about the emotion. Thus the ANS response contributes to arousal whereas the CNS response results in either approach (to stimuli that produce pleasant arousal) or avoidance or aggression (if the arousal is unpleasant).

THE AUTONOMIC NERVOUS SYSTEM

The ANS involves lower-order brain centers and also nerves in the spinal cord, which transmit impulses to various endocrine glands and smooth muscles, such as are contained in the heart and arteries. There are two divisions to the ANS, called the *sympathetic* and *parasympathetic* systems. These are coordinated so that in a given emotional state there is some combination of both in action.

Sympathetic behavior energizes one for strenuous action. Thus in a football game the body is "hyped up." Extra blood, carrying extra oxygen and fuel (blood sugar) is sent to the muscles. This means that the liver must release glycogen, the lungs must breathe more

---

* The process is not yet entirely clear. The thalamus, hypothalamus, limbic system, and other brain subdivisions are being studied.

deeply and rapidly, the heart must beat faster and more strongly, and blood pressure must rise. We can also notice dryness of the mouth, tightness of the stomach, moist palms, and gooseflesh.

The parasympathetic system tends to produce a calming or even a depressing effect, as when we are sorrowful at the death of a loved one. Accordingly, we have biological reactions somewhat the opposite of those produced by the sympathetic nervous system; we may experience a temperature drop, extreme lethargy, diminished rate and depth of breathing, and other symptoms.

### LEARNING AUTONOMIC RESPONSES

Autonomic responses appear to be the result of classical conditioning. For example, children appear to be highly aroused and even distressed by loud noises; such responses are apparently reflexive or inborn. Later, when they meet a barking dog, the sight and sound of it can result in a conditioned response, so that the child will be aroused at the sight of the dog even when it is not barking. This response may generalize to other stimuli, so that the child reacts not only to one dog, but to all dogs, and perhaps even to pictures of dogs.

In school a child may learn to fear a punitive teacher. This fear results in conditioning so that the sight of the teacher, the classroom, or even the thought of school produce anxiety. Again, a common anxiety is that produced by tests, or anything reminding one of tests.

Of course, positive emotions are learned in the same way, so that a display of dinnerware in a store window produces the pleasurable effect associated with food; and the word Mother, which is sometimes invoked by politicians, produces the trust and reassurance that one's own mother did.

In school a child may learn to fear a punitive teacher. This fear can be learned through observation; direct experience is not needed. Thus, fear of spiders may be generated in a child if he sees someone else showing fear, even though he himself has never been bitten.

ANS behavior is "automatic." That is, for all practical purposes it is not under conscious control. Once set in motion, it carries on by itself until a new stimulus causes the emotion to change.* Unfortunately, destructive emotions may continue long after their usefulness has passed. For example, you may experience anxiety for months after

---

* New research is giving us methods of dealing with this. Biofeedback, in which a person, through the use of electronic media, can see his blood pressure or other reactions, allows one to learn to control some autonomic responses. Of course, for years those skilled in Yoga have claimed to be able to exercise control by thought and concentration.

a dangerous situation such as a near-miss auto accident has occurred. Your heart may pound for some time, and you may have other symptoms. Indeed, it is possible in such situations for shock to set in.

Sometimes there are long-term aftereffects, and even more or less permanent anxiety, especially if stresses keep recurring. Excessive long-term anxiety can produce physiological damage. We wish to prevent traumatic happenings and to help children to deal with them when they do happen.

LEARNING TO RECOGNIZE EMOTIONS

The CNS consists of the brain, spinal cord, and nerves incoming from the sense organs and outgoing to the musculature. The thinking, or cognitive, activities are located in the CNS; hence we "know" that we are angry, afraid, or happy.

Sometimes one has to learn what emotion he is experiencing, as well as the stimuli that induce it. An interesting experiment by Schacter and Singer (1962) involved subjects who thought they were in a study to examine ways vitamins might affect vision. They were actually injected with adrenalin, which produces physiological effects of arousal. One subgroup of subjects was told to expect "side effects" from the "vitamins," and the effects described to them were those which adrenalin produces. A second group was misinformed about the nature of the side effects, and a third group was not told to expect side effects.

Each subject was asked to wait in a room with another person whom he assumed was also a subject, but who actually was a confederate of the experimenter. With some subjects, the confederate acted happy and exhilarated. With others, he showed anger and frustration. Thus differential social cues were supplied to the real subjects for them to consider as reasons for their feelings, although the feelings were really due to adrenalin.

Those who had been correctly informed of the effects they would experience were not particularly influenced by the behavior of the confederate. Those who had not been told to expect side effects, and those who had been misinformed about the effects, tended to feel and express emotions similar to those represented by the confederate — that is, anger or exhilaration. The study shows that we use whatever clues we can muster in order to interpret our emotions.

In a similar vein, clinicians have found that some of their work involves helping clients to understand the emotions they are experiencing; they must help clients also to learn what stimuli elicit those emotions, whether the emotions are appropriate or not, and how to handle emotion-arousing situations.

All of this has implications for the developing child. As parents or as teachers of the young child we may be involved in helping him sort out and differentiate how he feels. Unfortunately, since our culture discourages expression of such emotions as anger, we sometimes steer him wrongly. For example, a child who is having a temper tantrum may be told that he really is "just tired." Again, if we let him know that he isn't supposed to publicly show anger, we may find him denying his emotions or feeling guilt over them, with consequent damage to his psychological health. It would be more appropriate to help the child to recognize what his emotional state might truly be and to learn to express it in socially acceptable ways.

We will now examine classical conditioning, particularly with respect to the emotions. That examination may give us clues for dealing with both pleasant and unpleasant emotional states.

## Classical Conditioning

Most readers will have heard of Pavlov, who was among the first really to develop research on classical conditioning. Working with conditioned reflexes, which are innate or natural body movements or other physiological processes, Pavlov developed the first principles of conditioning. These have been elaborated upon, especially by Russian psychologists, who now claim that they can condition almost any aspect of the person.

In one of his initial experiments Pavlov placed food powder on the tongue of a dog to elicit salivation. He then paired the stimulus of the food powder with the ringing of a bell; eventually the dog would salivate to the sound of the bell alone.

Because emotions are physiological, we can study them from a classical conditioning frame of reference.

### DEFINITIONS

A *stimulus* is technically defined as a sensory input such as a light wave, pressure, or heat, but most writers use the source of that stimulus (a lamp, a pat on the back, a fire) as "stimuli." Stimuli can be internal, such as pain, hunger, or even one's own ideas, or they can be external. The function of a stimulus is to *elicit a response*. This means that the response follows automatically. It is not motivated, nor is it initiated by the individual; it is "drawn forth" by the stimulus. This should be carefully noted, since it is one of the major distinctions separating classical from operant conditioning.

A *response* is simply the behavior that results when a stimulus is presented. (There is circularity in these definitions, of course.) In classical conditioning the responses are usually physiological — movement, changes in blood pressure, contraction of the pupil of the eye, and so on — although cognitive processes can also be conditioned, as when we stop at the sight of an onrushing car or rise at the sound of a fire bell.

A given stimulus may elicit several simultaneous responses, and a given response may be elicited by a number of different stimuli. Furthermore, we can chain stimulus-response (S-R) bonds together, so that a response to one stimulus may itself become a stimulus for another response. An example might be walking, in which one step is the stimulus for the next.

THE CONDITIONING PROCESS

In the laboratory, we begin classical conditioning with an *unconditioned* stimulus (UCS), which elicits an *unconditioned* response (UCR). This simply means that the response occurs naturally in the presence of the stimulus. This response is usually a reflex, although in extended forms of conditioning it may have been learned. Thus, for example, if we shine a light into someone's eye, we get a pupillary contraction; the light is the unconditioned stimulus (UCS) and the contraction is the unconditioned response (UCR).

If we present a new stimulus about half a second before the UCS, in time the new stimulus elicits the response also, and we can drop the UCS from the situation. We now have a conditioned stimulus (CS), the new one; the former UCR is now a conditioned response (CR), since it occurs in response to the new stimulus. In our example we might introduce a buzzer together with the light. In time, the buzzer (CS) will elicit the same pupillary contraction (CR). Figure 3–1 shows diagrammatically how this occurs.

It should be noted that the CS-CR bond is not usually permanent. That is, if we use the buzzer to get the pupillary contraction frequently, in time the buzzer will no longer elicit that response. When this happens we say that *extinction* has occurred. This is important, for it provides us with a way to get rid of undesirable conditioning, as we shall see.

If we do want to make sure that conditioning continues, we must occasionally use the UCS together with the CS (that is, the light must

Figure 3–1.   *Classical Conditioning*

| Stage 1 | UCS $\longrightarrow$ UCR | |
| | (light) | (pupillary contraction) |
| Stage 2 | CS   +   UCS $\longrightarrow$ UCR | |
| | (buzzer)   (light) | (pupillary contraction) |
| Stage 3 | CS $\longrightarrow$ CR | |
| | (buzzer) | (pupillary contraction) |

be re-presented along with the buzzer). This is known as *reinforcement*.

Conditioning usually requires a number of trials, but if the situation is powerful enough, it can take place in one trial and may be very hard to extinguish. An example is the fear of airplanes which occurs after a crash.

An old but excellent illustration of the conditioning of emotional behavior is that of Watson and Rayner's (1920) work with a child and a white rat. Watson found that striking an iron bar to produce a loud noise would elicit a fear response from the child. He then introduced a rat at the same time he struck the bar and found that the child soon reacted with fear to the sight of the rat alone.

In conditioned responses we find *generalization*, both to other stimuli and to other responses. In an extension of Watson's work, one boy's fear generalized to other furry animals besides the rat, and even to his mother's fur coat (Jones, 1924). However, stimuli that are less similar to the original conditioned stimulus tend to elicit weaker responses. This gives us another means of dealing with conditioned responses, as we shall see when we discuss Wolpe's work.

Stimulus generalization is important in the school setting. Consider, for example, how early difficulties with some aspect of arithmetic may generalize to emotional reactions (as well as attitudes) toward mathematics of all kinds and at all levels; or how reading problems, correlated with emotional problems, may permeate the entire curriculum for a particular child. I am reminded of a child acquaintance who had spent some time in a nonpublic school where the teachers wore severe clothing and where the disciplinary measures were equally severe. When the child was entered in a public school, his teacher happened to wear clothing somewhat similar to that worn by his former teachers, and he immediately burst into tears and asked to go home. Here we have not only stimulus generalization but response generalization as well. Thus children who have experienced humiliation for failure to do well at a given school task may develop the same feelings about many school tasks, and accordingly any challenge may provoke anxiety, which can lead to lack of trying, withdrawal, physiological (psychosomatic) symptoms, or even severe mental health problems.

One other point must be made. One can be conditioned to words as well as to actual situations. It is thus not necessary to experience a real situation, so long as words carry ideas. Words have both denotative and connotative aspects. Consider the word "height." This means, *denotatively*, a distance from the level; it can refer to the height of a person, the height of ground, or the height at which an airplane flies. But I know one woman who has never been in a jet-liner because *connotatively* the idea of height means danger. And I recently watched men building a tall chimney for a power plant. Although I am not afraid of airplanes, I experienced a real twinge of anxiety watching the men raise the chimney, and "chimney" now connotes danger.

In the classroom, conditioning may occur without the teacher's intent or knowledge. Thus some children become conditioned to fear tests or even recitation in front of the class. It is part of our work as teachers to try to discover undesirable emotional conditioning and to alleviate it.

On the other hand, teachers want to make the school comfortable, exciting, and pleasurable for children, and we may be able to introduce some positive conditioning for that purpose.

## *Introducing Desirable Conditioning*

Because of both direct conditioning and generalization, and because of the fact that one CS can be hooked to a new stimulus to produce an extended CS-CR bond, we have opportunities to introduce desirable conditioning in the school and classroom. Essentially we provide as many stimuli as possible to elicit desired emotional responses. Since those stimuli are present when schoolwork is being done, we may expect that stimuli related to the school tasks will be pleasant also.

For example, although school is a place where children should employ effort in attempts to learn, there is every reason to provide an attractive physical environment just as we do in our homes. Thus newer schools use cheery colors, carpeting, interesting furniture, pictures on the wall, flowers, and all sorts of equipment, books, and media, which are attractive and which may stimulate pleasure, interest, and effort. In contrast, many rural and urban slum schools have broken or dirty windows, unlovely walls, floors, and windows, beat-up desks, and general dreariness.

Similarly, our choices of the media for instruction can perhaps be improved. The well-known *Sesame Street* is an example of how children will learn, turning on their television sets without reminder, since humor, color, songs, and the like are provided.

The teacher, too, can be a pleasant stimulus. It is almost axiomatic that the emotional tone of the class is set by the teacher. Thus his appearance, voice, vivacity, humor, accepting demeanor, and other personal variables induce desirable emotional responses.

Finally, learning activities can be fun. Although school is not supposed to be play, we all respond to learning activities framed as puzzles, challenges, games, and so on. Notice how quickly children at home learn to deal with numbers in such games as Monopoly, Rummy Royale, and others. Notice how vocabulary improves with Scrabble.

In summary, it is not only the content and tasks which cause children to enjoy school and learning. The presence of pleasure-eliciting stimuli, either directly or indirectly in the learning context, also helps to induce a desirable learning climate.

## Preventing Undesirable Conditioning

As teachers, we wish to provide experiences that do not lead to frustration, anxiety, anger, or fear. For example, if one were teaching football, which is after all a rough contact sport, he would wish to ensure maximum freedom from fear of injury by providing careful instruction in how to avoid injury, by providing adequate protective equipment, and by matching his players for size and ability. In teaching swimming, one might help children to avoid fear of water by providing flotation devices, teaching how to hold one's breath under water, and the like. In regard to tests, recitations, and similar class activities, one would try to ensure maximum success for the child and to introduce him to the situation gradually and with positive support.

It is better to prevent negative emotions than to try to deal with them after they have been established. Sometimes, however, such negative conditioning does occur.

## Dealing with Undesirable Conditioning

It is not hard to document the fact that much of what goes on in the school produces negative emotional tones in many children. Among the anxiety-producing situations are tests, threats of failure in a course, work that is too difficult, teachers with "negative personalities," inappropriate groupings, harsh discipline, and so on. Some readers may recall how they felt when passing the principal's office.

One of our students illustrates this point. She is a young lady from Brazil. In her case, a paper was not done quite well enough, so that it was necessary to ask her to resubmit it. Her reaction was not only one of discouragement but also of resentment. In an interview she said that although she thought the paper had some merit, it was treated without mention of any possible strong points. In fact, she thought, she might well drop out of further studies. Probing showed also that the atmosphere of a large university — competitive, somewhat impersonal, and in an alien culture — had caused her frustration, humiliation, loneliness, and discouragement. It can be seen that her feelings were the result not only of the actual criticism of her paper but of what she felt was an entirely unfeeling situation. As a result, steps were taken to try to help foreign students feel more at home, and we were again reminded of the need for positive as well as negative feedback.

Negative emotions can be specific to a situation, or they can be generalized. Among them are frustration, anger, resentment, fear, anxiety, and depression. What can be done once these emotions are acquired?

### EXTINCTION

The repeated pairing of the CS with the UCS causes the CS to elicit the same response as does the UCS. Should such pairing of stimuli *not* occur, so that the CS is called upon to elicit the CR *without* the reinforcement of the UCS, eventually the CS loses its power to elicit the CR. When this happens, extinction is said to have taken place.

One way to produce extinction is to engage frequently in the CS-CR situation but to ensure that the UCS is completely absent. The number of trials needed for such extinction varies. For example, if one has been attacked in the night by an intruder, such powerful conditioning may be produced by that single instance that it may last for years, even though the incident is never repeated. On the other hand, it does not take long for one to lose his fear of freeways once he begins using them.

Consider some of the following rather common instances. Children initially do not fear tests, but they do fear threatening adults. If a child, having taken a test, is then told he is stupid, lazy, and unacceptable, he will react to those remarks with anger, fear, or frustration; an instance or two of this kind will cause the test and probably any other stimuli connected with evaluation to produce the same emotions that the teacher's remarks did.

Another common example is that of "stage fright." If a child reciting in class is laughed at for being inept, any stimuli relating to recitations. will produce anxiety. If he is then forced to recite, his anxiety will get in his way and produce even poorer performance, which in turn increases the anxiety.

Still another instance can be seen in a recently integrated school. Suppose that a child from a minority group attempts to become friends with a person from the majority. Suppose, furthermore, that the majority group member rejects the minority child. Anger might well be the latter's reaction. After an instance or two of this sort the minority child might not only be angry at the majority group children but resent everything about the majority culture. It is obvious that the nature of a child's experiences with integration may confirm or increase any negative feelings between individuals of various racial groups; on the other hand, should initial experiences be successful, we might expect extinction of any negative attitudes originally present.

Finally, consider test anxiety again. To employ extinction, the teacher must try to make sure that the child will take tests when necessary, while making certain that he does not reinforce the child's anxiety by making negative comments. The teacher might emphasize the correct answers the child has made; he might praise the child's efforts; he might provide easy tests so that the child does well; he might help the child to study for the tests to enable him to make good marks; but the main thing is to avoid reinforcing negative feelings.

In many instances extinction cannot take place because people try to avoid the situations that frighten or humiliate them, and the response tendency does not erode unless used. Thus a child who is afraid of tests cannot lose his fear by simply refusing to take tests, and the child who is afraid of the water will not lose his fear by avoiding water. *Each needs to engage in the fearsome activity, but conditions must be arranged so that the fears are not reinforced.*

Sometimes people try to reduce anxiety, and partially succeed, through avoidance behaviors. This means that they seize upon activities that help them to deal with the anxiety, but not with the problem at hand. Thus children with fear of failure in school may resort to cheating; to rationalizing their failures as being the fault of the teacher; to trying to "psych out" the teacher so that the teacher answers his own questions; to playing ill; or to finding school "irrelevant." One can blame others, deny his own shortcomings, or even use superstition as ways of reducing anxiety, but those means are not constructive. Until the real difficulties are dealt with, the basic cause of the anxiety continues to exist.

University students have various devices for trying to reduce the pressures of exams. Some throw parties on the eve of the final exam on the theory that they will relax and therefore do better. Although they may relax on the night before, the old fear is still there on the day of the test. It would be much better to prepare for the exam, do as well as possible, and thus overcome the conditioned anxiety response.*

REINTERPRETING THE STIMULUS

We have considered stimulus generalization, in which stimuli that alone should not elicit emotions may do so because they are somewhat like the initial conditioned stimulus. In reinterpreting the stimulus for dealing with unpleasant emotions, we are trying to help the child discriminate between stimuli that might legitimately elicit a response and stimuli that should not do so. We are trying to work preventively as well as remedially.

For example, some snakes are poisonous; they usually have diamond-shaped heads. Other snakes are harmless or beneficial; they

---

* Anxiety has been portrayed as an undesirable emotional response. That view should be qualified, however. In some instances, a moderate degree of anxiety may facilitate learning and performance; this is sometimes known as "optimal anxiety." For example, I once had the opportunity to talk to Charles Laughton, at that time a screen and stage star of tremendous stature, possessor of numerous awards. Noting that Laughton gave some indication of anxiety in spite of his many triumphs, I queried him: Laughton replied that he deliberately tried to induce a moderate degree of anxiety before a performance, because otherwise, if he was too relaxed, he would put the audience to sleep. Similarly, the coach tries to get his team "up" for the game. But too strong or too continual anxiety interferes with performance as well as with mental health. Incidentally, complex performance is interfered with more than simple, well-learned performance.

have rounded heads. If we can help pupils to notice these differences, they should not react to round-headed snakes; on the other hand, fear of diamond-headed snakes is useful and should call for defensive maneuvers.

Similarly, small children are sometimes afraid of dogs. The neighborhood pet may have barked, jumped on the child, or even growled and showed his teeth. But most dogs are friendly. If we can show children that tail-wagging pups simply want to make friends, that some jumping is merely play, and that the dog can growl in mock ferocity, perhaps the child can discriminate between the really vicious animal and one that is not. Incidentally, one recommended procedure is to buy the child a small puppy. As the pup grows, its various behaviors will be displayed. By the time the dog is an adult, the child has learned to discriminate and no longer generalizes his fears.

In school the teacher can help the child learn to discriminate between normal rowdy behaviors and actual attempts at harm; between helpful criticism and negative evaluation of the child himself; between failing at a school task and failing as a person; and between good humor and derisive laughter.

## DESENSITIZING

In desensitizing, we are trying to change the response rather than the meaning of the stimulus. This may be done by building up a competing response that is more desirable than the original. Remember that one may make more than one response to a given stimulus, and that those responses may be quite different; also remember that as we deal with stimuli farther and farther in psychological distance from the original, the response strength decreases.

The first point may be illustrated by considering a child who wants to show you a drawing he has made, hoping for praise, but who may also not wish to show it, since he feels it is not good enough.

The second point may be illustrated by the same child's feeling that showing his drawing to his mother is less threatening than showing it to his teacher, and that showing it to the teacher is in turn less threatening than displaying the work on a bulletin board.

Let us look at some of Wolpe's (1958) work to understand how desensitizing can occur.* Wolpe believes that anxiety, a physiological (ANS) conditioned response to a stimulus, is at the root of much

---

* The term "desensitizing" is mine. Wolpe uses "reciprocal inhibition." What is really happening is that one builds a response incompatible with the undesirable response so the latter either does not occur or is weakened.

maladjustment. This results in behaviors designed to avoid the anxiety-producing stimulus; such behaviors may be maladaptive or even neurotic.

Wolpe argues that if a response that is incompatible with anxiety can be elicited in the presence of the anxiety-producing stimulus, the anxiety response should weaken and eventually disappear; the competing, inhibiting response should be elicited instead.

In therapy, three responses that are incompatible to anxiety are sometimes built up: aggression, relaxation, and the sexual response. We would probably agree that only relaxation responses would be suited to the school setting.

The therapist first finds a hierarchy of stimuli on the same continuum as the primary, anxiety-inducing stimulus, each less likely to draw a strong anxiety response. He can find this hierarchy through interviews. Thus if one were afraid of snakes, the therapist might find that the word *snake* induced less anxiety than a live snake. Similarly, a picture of a snake, a snake-skin shoe, or a stuffed snake might produce less anxiety.

He might then try to teach his client how to relax. A calm, secure environment, a comfortable mat or couch, a supportive therapist, the suggestion that one let his arms, head, and legs go limp — these can help relaxation.

At this point the least threatening stimulus is introduced — for example, the word *snake*. The client tries to remain relaxed while listening to this word. Eventually the word brings forth no anxiety reaction. It is then time to move up to the next stimulus, perhaps a picture of a snake. Again the client learns to remain relaxed. Eventually the entire hierarchy can be encompassed. (Actually, in much of this sort of therapy the client is asked to imagine a snake-skin shoe, and so forth, rather than being exposed to the real stimuli.) Finally the client is presumably desensitized to "snake anxiety": the anxiety response is inhibited and eventually should be extinguished.

The teacher, of course, is not a psychotherapist, yet he can deal with less severe problems in a quite analogous way. For example, consider stage fright. Some children are so anxious when asked to recite in public, play an instrumental solo, or take part in a drama (all conditioned stimuli) that they are not only emotionally upset (conditioned response), but their performance deteriorates badly. The teacher might try to provide a relaxing, supportive situation and introduce the child to the high-anxiety situation gradually. For example, the child might at first recite orally only to the teacher, being suitably encouraged and treated in a relaxing fashion. Later he might read to a study group of two or three nonthreatening classmates, and still later to the entire class. In the case of music he could play as part of a band or an orchestra, later as a member of a quartet, trio, or duet, and finally accomplish his solo.

There are two key elements in desensitizing. One is the provision of a nonthreatening situation, preferably with relaxation, and the other is a very gradual move toward the more threatening situations. Desensitizing includes more than learning to live with anxiety, however. It rests also on the ability to build up competing stimuli, in most instances, relaxation. It is necessary to proceed slowly, making certain that the student can tolerate each level before moving to the next. And of course it is absolutely necessary to avoid negative feedback, since that would only reinforce the anxiety and undo any good that had been done.

### SUPPORT AND MODELLING

It is interesting to see how often fear of snakes appears in studies dealing with the treatment of fear. Meichenbaum (1971) reports dealing with this fear in an extension of Wolpe's work, using modelling, verbalization, and self-rewarding statements. He dealt with a coping attempt which leads to the extinction of fear. This means that one must in a way "psych himself up" to engage in activities which he fears; otherwise extinction cannot take place.

In Meichenbaum's study, people with fears observed models who seemed to have no fear of snakes and who could pick them up and otherwise manipulate them. They also observed models who themselves showed initial fears, but who were gradually able to overcome them. The latter, or coping models, seemed to produce more beneficial effects in the fearful observers.

The observers were then asked to move toward harmless snakes and to try to nerve themselves to pick up the snakes. Verbalization was interesting. For example, Meichenbaum (1971, p. 300) reports a student saying

I have to pick up the snake. Okay, one step at a time. First, I'll put my hand in the cage and stroke it first, good. You feel a little cold, but not slimy like most people imagine. Lie still, so I can get a proper hold on you; first behind the head and now down by the tail. Now I have you, pick it up slowly in order not to injure it. Good, I've got you. You're a cute fellow.

\*     \*     \*

I'm going to make a deal with you. If you don't scare or hurt me, I won't scare or hurt you — Wait until I tell my mom. I was able to handle a snake for a full minute, she won't believe it. I'm so happy with myself, I was able to overcome my fear.

Modelling, of course, is not related merely to fears and anxiety; it can help in dealing with hostility and aggression, disgust (for example, among student nurses who dislike the sight and smell of blood), and of course the more positive emotions.

We should also consider two other aspects of getting pupils to engage in activities in which we want extinction to take place. One is the preparation of the pupil for what will happen. Thus the football coach engages his players in practice until they are as ready for a game as he can help them to be. He may use role-play by having one of his teams imitate the opposing team and its plays. He may also use films of games the other team has played and call attention to situations his team might anticipate. Psychologically, this is called *behavior rehearsal*, and it is an excellent technique for dealing with many pupil problems.

The second aspect is that of actual support. For example, if a child is afraid of dark places, perhaps his fears can be overcome if a friendly adult holds his hand while taking him through those places. Or what is even better, if a slightly older child who does not fear the dark can take him through, the support *plus* the modelling can be beneficial.

Since fears are caused not so much by the knowledge of what might happen as by the unknown, if one is given adequate preparation for what he will face, he can frequently muster the strength to face it.

## Conclusion

A case has been made for the relevance of classical conditioning to affective learning. Whether we are aware of it or not, this sort of learning does exist. All too frequently it is ignored or overlooked, and it is our contention that all of us should be more aware of it and begin to deal with it. Most of our efforts should be devoted to promoting desirable emotional reactions; at the very least we can act to ensure that school tasks do not produce negative emotions. When negative emotions do occur, we, either by ourselves as teachers, or with the help of psychologists or counsellors, can do something positive about it.

Another important kind of learning is operant conditioning. Indeed, B. F. Skinner (1972) sold over a million copies of his book *Beyond Freedom and Dignity*, which is based on a translation of operant principles into our social lives. The next chapter will deal with that form of learning and briefly with the points of view which strong proponents to it have taken.

## SUGGESTION FOR FURTHER READING

Travers, R. M. W. *Essentials of Learning.* New York: Macmillan, 1963.

# Chapter 4

# OPERANT CONDITIONING
# AND AFFECTIVE BEHAVIOR

*Judge Thyself who was right — Thou or he who questioned Thee then? Remember the first question; its meaning, in other words, was this: "Thou wouldst go into the world, and art going with empty hands, with some promise of freedom which men in their simplicity and their natural unruliness cannot even understand, which they fear and dread — for nothing has ever been more insupportable for a man and a human society than freedom. . . ."*

*Instead of taking men's freedom from them, Thou didst make it greater than ever! Didst Thou forget that man prefers peace, and even death, to freedom of choice in the knowledge of good and evil? Nothing is more seductive for man than his freedom of conscience, but nothing is a greater cause of suffering. And behold, instead of giving a firm foundation for setting the conscience of man at rest for ever, Thou didst choose all that is exceptional, vague and enigmatic; Thou didst choose what was utterly beyond the strength of men. . . .*

— FYODOR DOSTOYEVSKY

The setting for this quotation is a hypothetical conversation between the Grand Inquisitor of the Church and a figure whom we presume to be Jesus Christ returned to earth. Christ is being berated for promising men freedom. The Inquisitor takes the position that for their individual and collective good, people must be given direction and must be controlled, even to the point where some deception is used.

In effect, he is saying that people want an ordered society; they are happier when they are told what they should and should not do and how they should do it. They value food, shelter, peace, and order rather than freedom, which confuses them. Life is easier and more pleasant if one is not faced with decisions and need not develop his own conscience; one must be protected from both his fellow men and himself. The humane way, then, is not to give people freedom, but to direct and control.

That such feeling exists today is attested by Kaufman (1973), who has coined the term *decidophobia* — fear of making decisions — and has shown that some of us use various strategies to avoid making major decisions — among them adherence to religion, drifting, allegiance to a movement, moral rationalism, and even marriage (there are ten strategies in all). So it may be argued that people, at least many of them, want to be controlled.

Again, B. F. Skinner (1973) argues that our attempts at freedom, exemplified in education by the free schools, does not pay off for either the pupil or his society. Skinner's argument may be interpreted as follows.

What may be called the struggle for freedom is really a struggle to escape punishment or coercion. Education, in common with other institutions, too long used such methods, which were neither humane nor productive. On the other hand, simply the removal of aversive stimuli (that is, punishment, threat) does little to ensure that pupils will learn. Although pupils should enjoy learning because they see its value, unfortunately that may not be the case. After all, freedom is an illusion. Behavior is always under control of its consequences. When teachers refuse to control pupils, other environmental factors assume control instead.

Skinner (1973, p. 16) then points out that attempts to allow the child to simply develop, with the teacher stimulating or guiding, overlook two points. One is that a lot of teaching is needed for the child to learn from his physical and social environment. The other is that the child must be provided with knowledge that will be relevant to the future as well as the present; this calls for teachers being willing to say what we believe students will need to know in the future, allowing for individual differences.

The natural, logical outcome of the struggle for personal freedom in education is that the teacher should improve his control of the student rather than abandon it. The free school is no school at all. Its philosophy signalizes the abdication of the teacher. The teacher who understands his assignment and is familiar with the behavioral processes needed to fulfill it can have students who not only feel free and happy while they are being taught but who will continue to feel free and happy when their formal education comes to an end. They will do so because they will be successful in their work (having acquired useful productive repertoires), because they will get on well with their fellows (having learned to understand themselves and others), because they will enjoy what they do (having acquired the necessary knowledge and skills), and because they will from time to time make an occasional creative contribution toward an even more effective and enjoyable way of life. Possibly the most important consequence is that the teacher will then feel free and happy too.

Thus control is desirable, but it must be exerted in a benign way; instead of using threat or coercion or harping on the pupil's derelictions or weaknesses, we must learn to focus on and reward the pupil's successes and desirable behaviors.

## A Point of View

We now need to consider the relationship of operant conditioning to the affective domain. Operant conditioning is based on the belief that behavior is governed by its consequences, or by expectations of its consequences. (Behavior need not always be governed by the *present* environment, however, since much of our learning was controlled previously, by our parents and teachers.) A strict behaviorist places most of these controls in the environment; that is, we act and are then rewarded or punished by elements in the situation, causing our behavior to recur, or not, as the case may be. It is easy to see, then, that through conditioning experiences, we anticipate reward (pleasure) or punishment (fear, anxiety, depression). A feeling tone and an attitude are developed as the result of a given behavior.

Skinner (1971) explains that values, too, are the result of operant conditioning, in the sense that they accompany behavior and are essentially generalizations of our expectations of the effects of our behaviors. If that is so, then changing behavior appropriately will have positive consequences, and we will value the changed behavior.

If, for example, being kind to others pays off in the reinforcements they provide us, we will continue to be kind to them because our expectations are pleasurable. Presumably we would begin to value being kind to others. But on the other hand, should our kindness cause others to take advantage of us, our expectations would become negative, and both our behavior and values would change accordingly.

There is some question, of course, as to when one generalizes a number of specific experiences and develops a value. Teachers worry about whether pupils are working merely for grades or other rewards or because they find value in the work itself. This is a very real problem, and it is compounded when we use such extrinsic rewards as candy or tokens to get a child involved in his schoolwork. (Of course, unless we get him involved in some way, he has no chance to find any intrinsic values in it.)

How can one tell whether values or attitudes have changed, or whether the child is merely "playing the game" for the external rewards we are using? One way to tell is to cease the rewards. If the child then drops his desirable behavior, it seems clear that his attitudes have not altered. But even if he continues even after we have ceased to reinforce him, can we be certain his attitudes or values have changed? Not necessarily. Some other reinforcers may be operating. Perhaps because the child now attends to his schoolwork his grades have improved. In that event, it is possible that now his parents are pleased and are praising or rewarding him.

But if a pupil studies voluntarily even when it is not required because he is interested and finds the work rewarding in itself, we can assume a value change. And this does occur, as any teacher can testify. Would that it happened to all children.

Helping such value changes to take place will be considered further when we discuss reinforcers and consider the concept of *functional autonomy* later in this chapter.

Thus operant conditioning is related to emotions, interests, attitudes, and values. They are subject to control, and some control, at least, seems necessary.

It would seem, then, that our job as teachers is to involve the child in appropriate activities by using whatever reinforcers we can. But we then must go further and help him to find intrinsic rewards, hence values, in the activities themselves. If we cannot do so, there is every likelihood that once school is out, the activities will be abandoned with relief.

Before we get further into theory, let us provide an illustration.

## A Student Teacher Discusses Don

Don is four years and five months of age, and as far as can be determined, is above average in intelligence. He is basically healthy, having no more than an occasional cold. In weight and height he compares with the average of the class. Usually he is dressed neatly and cleanly, although his clothing is never out of the ordinary. Don is a boy, thus, who might not even be noticed in class — that is, until one takes his behavior into account.

On the whole, I would have to interpret his behavior as extremely attention-seeking. I shall cite a few examples of this so that it will be more clear to the reader. Whenever the teacher is sitting on a chair in front of the class, Don runs to sit in front of her and holds on to her leg. If the class is asked to sit and wait for the teacher because she is still busy at her desk, Don runs to the desk and will not sit until told to do so at least two or three times. He just grins when the teacher tells him at first and does not move until she actually yells at him. Once while the class was making jello, each child had a chance to stir it. After being told specifically to be sure to hang on to the spoon, he just let go of it and let it drop into the bowl and sink down into the jello. On another occasion, the class was making construction paper figures. Each child was told to take one piece of paper and make one figure. Don took five pieces of paper and made five figures.

I felt that in interpreting Don's behavior, the teacher's response should be taken into consideration, for she seems to respond to and thus reinforce every activity that Don is doing. If two or three people are doing something wrong, Don is the one that is rebuked. A few other examples follow.

When the class was going to make jello, the girls were supposed to move to the activity room and the boys to remain seated except Mark, who was to help the teacher and was then given something to carry. Don immediately wanted to "help" and the teacher gave *him* something to carry. While doing "jumping jacks" some of the boys had difficulty coordinating the movements. Don was one of them, so the teacher said out loud that he was doing them wrong, and went to help him while she gave no help to the others. Occasionally when the group is sitting together, Don moves and sits under a table. When the teacher notices him, she yells at him to get out. When he refuses, she goes to pull him out while the class laughs and giggles.

Thus I think it can be seen that Don's activities which are attention-seeking are getting the responses desired and are thus being reinforced.

The teacher had apparently been told by a welfare psychologist to treat the boy as he was treated at home — that is, to yell at him if he misbehaved and not let him get away with anything. However, I decided to adopt the opposite technique with the little fellow, and ignore him.

On the first day of my teaching the class, Don acted up as usual, hanging on to my leg, talking out of turn, and so forth. I ignored this until he got to be really bad. Then I took him aside and said that as long as he continued to act up I would not consider him a part of the class and would not even recognize that he was there. He followed me around and I pretended he wasn't there. He continued to act up that day and I continued to ignore him. The next day he did not do as many things out of line. Once when he acted up during a lesson, I waited until the lesson was over, took him aside, and reminded him again of what I was doing and why I was doing it. One day while the class was putting on a dramatization, I told the class that those talking out of turn or trying to get ahead of someone so that they could act first would lose their turn. Eventually Don did both. When he did, I said "Someone has just lost his turn," and nothing more. When it came to the end, Don wanted his turn. I took him aside while the class was doing something else, and explained again why he got no turn and why he would continue not to get any if he continued to act the way he did. I thus took away not only his uncalled-for chances for attention, but his regular chances in the curriculum structure when he acted in a manner that disturbed the class.

He is becoming progressively less of a problem for me, although his bad behavior has not completely ceased. However, I feel that this is a successful way to deal with him, for the cooperating teacher still treats him in her usual way, always paying attention, and he continues to act up consistently for her. (Ringness 1968, pp. 317–18, 331–32)

This student teacher did indeed reduce Don's attention-seeking behavior by not reinforcing it. However, she did not do all that she could have done; for example, she could have reinforced any desirable behavior he might have shown. Furthermore, since the cooperating teacher was not cooperating in this instance, Don was probably learning to discriminate between the two teachers rather than changing his behavior in earnest. If both teachers *and* Don's mother had treated Don in the same way, he might have been expected to learn behaviors and attitudes such as respect for the rights of others, cooperation, and how better to deal with his need for attention.

## How Does Operant Conditioning Operate?

The terms *stimulus* and *response* have the same meaning in operant and in classical conditioning. *Reinforcement*, however, is different. In *classical* conditioning, *reinforcement* refers to the presentation of the UCS along with the CS, thus strengthening the power of the CS to elicit the CR. In *operant* conditioning, however, the subject is motivated. Reinforcement is the provision of a suitable reward, related to that motivation, *after* the desired behavior occurs.

In other words, in *classical* conditioning, the stimulus *elicits* (calls forth) a response; but in *operant* conditioning, the behavior is motivated: the subject wishes to *operate* on the environment to gain a desired end. We thus say that the response is *emitted* — that is, initiated by the subject. If the subject emits no desired responses, operant conditioning obviously cannot strengthen the response tendency. In that event it becomes necessary to try other tactics.

Humanely, we usually try to reinforce appropriate behavior rather than punish inappropriate behavior. When we do need to reduce inappropriate behavior, we prefer to use *extinction* rather than punishment. This is done by making certain that inappropriate responses are not rewarded, as the student teacher did by ignoring Don's attention-seeking behaviors. Occasionally, however, we may be forced to cause behavior to be *inhibited* through punishment, as when Don lost his turn to act.

OBTAINING DESIRED BEHAVIOR

The intent is to reinforce desired behavior when it occurs, so that the likelihood of its recurrence will increase. We will illustrate with an example which has been filmed (Skinner, 1939). In the film, B. F. Skinner places a hungry pigeon in a cage containing a food trough which rises with food pellets when he presses an electrical switch. He also uses a buzzer to attract the pigeon's attention to the trough. In one experiment he desired the pigeon to turn in a circle. That is something a pigeon *can* do but *does not normally do* in search of food.

Skinner waited until the pigeon made the beginning of a turn. At that moment he pressed the switch, the buzzer sounded, and food was provided. The pigeon ate a little, thus being reinforced for the turning movement, although it is doubtful that the pigeon realized that in the way humans would.

The next time Skinner waited until the pigeon had moved further into a turn and then reinforced that behavior. Eventually he got the pigeon to make complete turns, always by waiting until the pigeon moved a little closer to the desired end behavior. The gradual approximation of the desired end behavior is said to be *shaped* by the experimenter.

Now we can state some of the principles involved in reinforcement.

1. The subject must be motivated. Skinner's pigeons were hungry when he worked with them. (In Don's case, a prominent motive was to seek attention, although of course he had other motives as well.)

2. The reinforcement must be related to the motive. The pigeon was fed. (In Don's case, the student teacher might have paid attention to him when he did something she approved of. For example, if he waited his turn at the bubbler, she might have praised him for being patient. When he studied, she might have smiled at him. Unfortunately, she did nothing to reinforce desirable behavior, but concentrated on reducing his annoying ways.)

3. The reward must be contingent upon emission of the desired behavior. If Skinner's pigeon had not begun to turn, he would not have rewarded it. Sometimes with animals the behavior never is emitted, or if it is, it is so infrequent that shaping is very difficult. But with humans, we can ask for what we want. (In Don's case the cooperating teacher was unfortunately rewarding him for the undesirable behaviors consistently. She was reinforcing, but not for the behavior she would have preferred.)

4. Reinforcement should be provided immediately, each time the behavior occurs, until it is well-instituted. In this way the reinforcement becomes associated with the behavior. (This is one reason Skinner has pushed programmed instruction; the almost inevitable success in learning the small steps is considered reinforcing to the student.) As we shall see, once the behavior is well established the rewards can be offered at intervals rather than every time the behavior occurs; still later, they may be dropped entirely.

Since reinforcement is aimed at causing a behavior to take place, *positive reinforcement,* or reward, is easy to understand. But what is *negative reinforcement?* It is simply the removal of an aversive stimulus. In laboratory experiments a rat may be placed on an electric grid and mildly shocked until it performs a desired act. The removal of the shock reinforces the bar-pressing, or whatever behavior we are after.

Human beings institute the positive behavior of shower-taking and using a deodorant to remove the negative stimulus of B.O. They fasten their seat belts to avoid an annoying buzzer. Or they put on an overcoat to avoid the negative stimulus of being cold.

People differ in what they consider reinforcing, and individuals differ from time to time. The teacher has many reinforcers at hand, but often fails to consider them; he also tends to feel that schoolwork should be self-reinforcing and that students should not be "paid for working." But when students fail to find their work reinforcing in itself, and when teacher approval or grades are not reinforcing enough, we can expect turned-off students, truants, dropouts, non-learners, and other alienated young people.

Let us consider a few of the reinforcers that do exist in most schools. (Creative teachers may be able to devise many more.)

#### EXTERNALLY ADMINISTERED REINFORCERS

1. Concrete reinforcers: rewards such as candy, food, prizes, and toys; tokens which can be exchanged for material goods or privileges; parties; permission to take things home from school; and the like.
2. Recognition: award pins, newspaper write-ups, football sweaters, uniforms, trophies.
3. Social reinforcers: expressions of approval, praise, friendship, smiles, pats on the back.
4. Positive feedback: marks, report cards, comments on papers, scholarships, participation in science fairs.
5. Miscellaneous reinforcers: being allowed to sit with a friend, time out to do what one prefers, field trips, movies.

These reinforcers are normally administered by the teacher. There is evidence that tokens, points, or other reinforcers are equally well administered by the pupils themselves, however. Thus Goodlet and Goodlet (1969) compared self- and external-administration of reinforcement in controlling the disruptive behavior of three ten-year-olds and found both methods effective. Lovitt and Curtiss (1969) and Glynn (1970) also found self-administration and contingency-determination (pupil determination of when they are to be reinforced) to enhance academic performance.

#### SELF-REINFORCEMENT

Once one has formed a value, acting in accordance with that value may be reinforcing in itself. Thus one feels pleasure in improving his golf game, even though he is not competing with anyone else. Or he feels good when he works for civil rights or Women's Liberation, even though he may be subjected to abuse by others. We continually monitor our actions, and we have feelings of pleasure or disgust as we meet or fail to meet our own standards. Presumably this is the reinforcement level we should all strive to meet.

It may help to think of levels of reinforcement, ranging from the concrete through social reinforcement to attaining one's values. You may wish to consider the relationship of such a progression to Kohlberg's progression of moral attainment (Chapter 2).

When we are infants, we need food, warmth, and comfort — and love. As we develop, we associate our parents with such creature comforts, and their smiles, praise, or frowns become social reinforcers. Later, as we internalize values, we may become self-reinforcing. (Probably in actual practice we respond to a combination of these forms of reinforcement.)

Some children do not respond to social reinforcers, nor do they have values that are preferred by the school. This may happen for a variety of reasons, such as inadequate child care during infancy and early childhood, a neglecting or hostile family, or a culture whose values differ from those of the school. Many children from lower socioeconomic levels seem not to value education; some view the street hustler as their ideal of attainment; many of them are disruptive. In order for the school to function, a measure of control over these children must be exerted.

One technique teachers can use with children who are not motivated by teacher comments, marks and grades, and so on, is to work with them on a schedule in which candy, tokens which can be exchanged for small gifts or privileges, and similar concrete reinforcers are paired with teacher praise, a pat on the back, and other social reinforcers. Before long the child should respond to the latter, and the former can be dropped.

In the long run, of course, we hope that the child will find value in his work, enjoy success, develop an appropriate value system, and thereby reinforce himself for his efforts. Allport (1961) uses the concept of *functional autonomy* to explain that one may initially engage in an activity for one reason but find satisfaction in that activity and continue it for other reasons. For example, the son of a physician might enter medicine primarily to please his father, but long after Dad has passed away, the son may continue because of the satisfaction he has gained in being a doctor, satisfaction that goes far beyond the prestige and material advantages of the profession. Similarly, a required course taken for the eventual reinforcement of a degree may awaken interest and be pursued for its own sake. When one has internalized the expectations of reinforcement for a given behavior, we can say that he then values the behavior and will reinforce himself with feelings of satisfaction when he so performs it.

SOME OTHER ASPECTS OF REINFORCEMENT

Earlier we made the point that people differ in what they think is reinforcing. For example, one child, bright but not working very hard, agreed with his teacher that if she would permit gum-chewing during the last fifteen minutes of the school day, he would make more effort to study. Although the teacher felt that she was being had, she decided to give it a try. The next day the boy brought chewing gum for the entire class, and because he studied well, everyone could chew for fifteen minutes. This became the thing to do, and the students not only had the reinforcement of the gum, but of the peer approval engendered by bringing a treat when it was their turn.

Again, a mathematics teacher in a deprived area of Los Angeles County found that his students became highly motivated when he began marking homework, tests, and so on with "money" grades; a top paper might bring a grade of fifty dollars, a good paper twenty dollars, and so on. The grades could be summed up so that on Friday the students could "buy" a free Coke, time off from class, or other things they desired. It wasn't long before the students were keeping their own books as a check on the teacher. And it wasn't long before they simply enjoyed "earning money" and neglected to collect their earned prizes. And why not? Their parents were highly concerned with earning a living. Even symbolic money reinforces us.

Teachers tend to wonder whether students will simply work for the reinforcers and discontinue when they are no longer paid off. They also wonder whether such payoff is not immoral. The concept of functional autonomy partially answers this question. It must also be noted that in a sense, praise, marks, promotions, and so on are also payoffs, although with many children they do not work, especially if the child fails to attain good marks. And it is true that especially with dull or difficult work, more immediate reinforcement is needed. Since one cannot gain satisfaction in the work itself until he does the work, sometimes extra motivational aids are required. And when the teacher threatens students with failure, lack of promotion, or other dire consequences, he will almost surely produce even more negative feelings in those students.

Teachers also worry about what might happen if children are not all treated alike — for example, some receive concrete reinforcements and others do not. If all children are treated as individuals, however, and if each is given a chance to gain the rewards he wishes, there is not much likelihood that cries of unfairness will be heard.

## SCHEDULES OF REINFORCEMENT

When we are trying to shape desired behavior we begin with immediate, continuous reinforcement, when that is possible. Every time we find a child doing something desirable, we reinforce it if we can. But as the behavior becomes more habitual, we drop off the frequency to every third or fourth time, or even to random reinforcement. This not only maintains the behavior, but seems to work better than when reinforcement is provided on a fixed schedule or according to a fixed ratio of reinforcements to desired behaviors.

There may come a time when reinforcers do not reinforce as well as they originally did. This may be the result of satiation. To illustrate, one might do a certain amount of work to earn a chocolate malted milk. He might not work quite so hard for a second. As for a third . . .

There are two answers to satiation. One is to seek another kind of reinforcer. But we can also use deprivation — withholding reinforcers for a time. For example, it has been shown that children provided with too much social reinforcement, such as praise, begin to slack off, and the praise becomes somewhat meaningless to them. Withholding praise for a time produces renewed attempts to earn it.

It should also be noted that reinforcement should be provided only for real accomplishment. The child who achieves an *A* for little effort does not prize the mark as much as the child who has been challenged and has had to put forth real effort.

REDUCING INAPPROPRIATE BEHAVIOR

The best way to reduce inappropriate behavior is to prevent it from being reinforced. This leads to extinction, just as in classical conditioning. Don's student teacher ignored him when he was seeking attention by clinging to her legs, trying to get ahead of others in drama, and so on. And as she said, his inappropriate behavior began to decrease while she was teaching.

Unfortunately, the cooperating teacher inadvertently continued to reinforce Don's attention-seeking, so that Don learned to discriminate between the two teachers. Thus he acted appropriately for the student teacher but not for the cooperating teacher.

When children misbehave, it is often because they have been reinforced by their peers. Children laugh at the class clown and admire the troublemaker — or at the very least, they pay attention to him. One of the techniques that works in such instances is to have a "time-out room" for the troublemaker: any room in which he can be placed alone and which is unstimulating and nonreinforcing. When the child is ready to return and cooperate, he is allowed to do so. Notice that this is not the same as punishment, since his return is contingent upon his own readiness to participate in class willingly.

Now let us consider *punishment* itself. Punishment is the provision of unpleasant consequences for the commission of an act. It is aimed at producing *inhibition* of behavior, whereas reinforcers are aimed at initiating and maintaining behavior. If punishment is severe enough and consistent, and if the punitive agent is always present, punished behavior should not recur.

But there are problems with punishment. One is that the motivation for the improper behavior is not changed, so that when the punishing agent is absent, the behavior may resume. If there are no squad cars in sight, drivers are inclined to speed; when police are present, everyone drives cautiously. Accordingly, some states have used wooden mock-ups painted to look like squad cars to slow people down.

A second problem is that punishment does not ensure desired alternative behavior. That will occur only when the desired behavior is known and is reinforced. If one does not know what he should do, punishment can only immobilize him.

A third problem is that punishment may only lead to learning to escape the punishment. Some drivers are now installing electronic devices in their cars to warn them of police radar. Children learn to cheat on tests in order to avoid poor grades. They learn to flush their cigarettes down the john when the washroom door opens unexpectedly.

Again, when too much punishment is used, one may learn negative emotions and attitudes, such as feeling inferior, becoming guilt-ridden, having a negative self-concept, disliking teacher and school, and becoming resentful and frustrated. The punitive classroom also tends to cause some children to scapegoat, taking out their hostilities toward the teacher by being unkind to weaker children, or even vandalizing the classroom.

And last but not least, punishment is aimed in some way at hurting the offender. As such, this technique is inhumane.

Sometimes punishment *is* necessary. When a child is excessively aggressive or hostile, hurts others, or takes dangerous chances, it may be necessary. But on the whole, it is not the preferred method of dealing with inappropriate behavior.

## Behavior Modification

"Behavior modification" is a name for a number of techniques aimed at eliminating undesired behaviors and reinforcing desired ones. Behavior modification goes beyond operant conditioning per se, in that it may utilize imitation or modelling, behavior rehearsal, or other techniques; nevertheless, reinforcement principles are prominent in most behavior modification attempts. Because behavior modification is a powerful tool, and because it is a deliberate attempt at control, a word about ethics may be needed.

### ETHICAL CONSIDERATIONS

Some students feel that control of behavior is immoral. They anticipate 1984 Big-Brother results and are afraid that individual freedom and uniqueness may be sacrificed. One should not fear behavior modification per se, however, but the ethical or unethical use of its techniques. It is true, of course, that like any other teaching technique, it can be misapplied.

We should note that in *any* social interaction, reinforcement of a feeling or a behavior takes place, whether by design or not. Whenever we talk with anyone, sit with anyone, or have any other transaction with him, our feelings, thoughts, and behaviors are modified in more positive or negative directions — and so are his. Thus when we use behavior modification we are only making more explicit our intent, and are carefully observing the effects of any reinforcements which are taking place.

It is also necessary to recognize that teachers are charged with responsibility for what goes on in the classroom. The question is not whether to control, but in what ways and how much. Research and experience show that the permissive teacher accomplishes relatively little and that pupils may be confused and frustrated (for example, Lewin, Lippitt, and White, 1939; Heil et al., 1962). Summerhill, A. S. Neill's famous experimental school, was found good for some students but not for all, and even in Summerhill there was control, administrated by the consensus of school meetings.

Furthermore, one can and should reinforce behaviors that actually enhance individuality. We can encourage individuality by reinforcing creative efforts, originality, and evaluative thinking.

SOME BASIC PRINCIPLES

1.  In most instances we are trying both to reduce inappropriate behavior and institute desirable behavior.
2.  The inappropriate behavior to be reduced is carefully observed for frequency and the conditions under which it occurs. Thus if a child frequently bothers other children, one wants to know how often he does it, when, what he does, and so on. A chart of such behavior is kept, thus providing baseline data against which progress can be assessed.
3.  One tries to see what is reinforcing the undesirable behavior. Is the child being laughed at? Surreptitiously encouraged?
4.  One tries to determine more appropriate behavioral objectives. Those objectives are discussed with the child, and he is encouraged to accept them as alternatives.
5.  The contingencies are stated. (Thus with Don, the student teacher said that when he sought attention inappropriately, she would ignore him. She might also have said that when he did certain things which she approved, she would reinforce him in certain ways.)
6.  One then consistently reinforces the child for his appropriate behaviors.
7.  Post-treatment data is gathered at intervals to see how the treatment is working. If it is not working, perhaps other reinforcers or some modification of the technique should be tried.

Caution! This isn't always as easy as it sounds. A teacher may need to consult a school psychologist, guidance counselor, or other experienced person. Things don't always turn out as expected. For instance, one of my colleagues is fond of the following story. A suburban housewife had two ten-year-old sons who were wonderful in most respects, except that they swore terribly. Upon consulting a psychologist, she was given the advice to treat them kindly when not swearing, but not to spare the rod when they did. One morning son number one came down to the kitchen. "And what would you like for breakfast, Dear?" asked his mother.

"I'd like some of the g—— d—— cornflakes," he remarked. Immediately he was heavily swatted in the appropriate place.

Seeing the second son watching from the head of the stairs, the mother again asked "And what would *you* like to eat this morning?"

"I don't know," he replied, "but it sure as h—— won't be any of those g—— d—— cornflakes."

## THE CASE OF THE HIGH SCHOOL
## ENGLISH CLASS

McAllister et al. (1969) discuss what happened with a young teacher who asked for consultative help in controlling her classroom. After two months with the students, she felt that she had some rapport but that they were doing rather poorly and did not always behave well. She was particularly bothered by the fact that sometimes students would talk without permission or turn around to look at persons behind them. It was decided to deal with each of these behaviors separately.

Baseline data were collected by observers. This consisted of keeping track minute by minute of when transgressions took place. A control classroom, in which the teacher behaved as usual, and an experimental room, in which she changed her tactics, were then subjected to study.

In the experimental room the teacher was instructed to reprimand *individual* students for talking without permission; thus she might say "John, please be quiet!" She was not to threaten or punish, but was to praise the *group* when possible by saying "Thank you for being quiet," or something similar. She worked on the students' talking without permission for 26 days and then compared her results with the baseline. In the next part of the experiment, the teacher worked on the students' turning around without permission.

The experiment was successful. The talking, and later the turning around, decreased in the experimental class as compared to the control class. The teacher became quite used to recording behavior, and stated that although keeping records and using reinforcing statements was somewhat burdensome, the resulting class behavior more than compensated for the extra effort.

The teacher was not left alone during the experiment. From time to time observers would visit the classroom to show her when she used reinforcers appropriately or failed to do so when she could have. Such feedback is often necessary, for the teacher is frequently inexperienced in this technique and is sometimes too busy to evaluate her behaviors as she goes along. (We might also note that, as Klein [1971] has shown, teachers are reinforced and shaped by pupils, quite unwittingly on the part of both. When pupils respond positively, so do teachers.)

### DUCK CALLS AND KITCHEN CLOCKS

A third-grade teacher had a noisy class which did not respond to appeals for quieter study. She discussed her problem with a consultant, who helped her to develop a behavior modification plan. First, the teacher obtained an ordinary clock-type kitchen timer. She also needed a device for making an unusual noise — and her husband provided her with his duck call!

The teacher explained to her class that the noise level was often too high for good working conditions, and that whenever she felt that to be the case, she would use the duck call to signal them. She demonstrated with a "quack, quack," which the children thought was very funny. She also told the pupils that she would set the kitchen timer and that for each ten minutes of acceptable quiet, she would give them an extra minute of recess.

The plan worked. For a short time the pupils had fun getting her to use the duck call, of course. But shortly quiet reigned. Before long the pupils were earning an extra fifteen minutes of recess, which the teacher thought was worth it, in view of the fact that better study conditions were now habitual.

Before long the timer and the duck call were discarded, and pupils began to shush each other whenever the room became noisy. Although absolute quiet was never demanded, the class itself felt the advantage of reasonable silence for school tasks.

### NOW LET'S CONSIDER A PROBLEM

A certain large city high school had many school-skippers. Some would come to school for part of the day and sneak out at noon.

Others might take whole days off. The school developed a policy of suspending the truants from class, so that for every three days they were absent, they were not allowed back for three days. Truancy continued.

It does not take much knowledge of reinforcement to see that not only was the school reinforcing truancy by rewarding the culprits with extra time off, but that any negative student attitudes were being reinforced. When that was realized, teachers began to make extra efforts to show the absentees that they were glad when the students were present. Furthermore, students were given help in making up missed work. These techniques did not solve all the problems, of course, but did cut down on some of the truancy.

It is surprising how frequently behaviors are shaped by people who are actually trying to reduce them. Consider the child who throws temper tantrums. Suppose he is in the grocery store with his mother and sees a candy bar he wants. The mother refuses to buy it, whereupon the child begins to reach for it, to cry, or to otherwise make a scene. The mother still refuses, speaks harshly, threatens punishment. The child makes a bigger scene — and the mother gives in and purchases the candy bar!

What has happened is clear. The mother has shaped up the temper tantrum. The child has learned that if he is offensive enough, he will get what he wants.

We have seen the same thing in campus protests. We have had them in regard to racial issues, conditions for teaching assistants, war in Vietnam, and other reasons. In most instances students have begun by trying to make their points of view clear to administrators controlling the point of discord. Now, one would think that it would be simple and desirable to hold dialogues with the students, make changes where possible, and try to explain when such changes were not possible. Such actions would reinforce appropriate behaviors — namely, the use of the democratic process in changing the views of the electorate and the use of due process of law.

But this has not always been the case. In some instances students had no real hearing from officials, and in fact were sometimes threatened or punished. Being frustrated, the students became angry and resorted to picketing, rock throwing, and fire bombing. Attention *was* paid to *that*. Officials listened and sometimes made changes.

This account has oversimplified the situation somewhat, since some professional agitators can never be satisfied and continue to find issues of even the most trivial kind. But the vast majority of students respond well to dialogue, explanation, and reasonable change. They only become a mob when mob tactics seem needed to force change.

(To give another example, it was not until black people became militant that their cries were heeded.)

Since most readers of this book will become teachers, it is worth remembering that *when undesirable behavior takes place, it may be we who are shaping it.*

## Behavioristic Humanism

Operant principles work best with human beings when there is active understanding by the learner of what is being attempted and when he agrees that such changes are desirable. Not only is this more effective, but it seems obviously more ethical. Wivett (1970) found that there are greater changes through behavior therapy when the subject attributes the changes to himself rather than to external conditions. Again, Blackwood (1970) points out that behavior modifications can reduce misbehaviors, but that they may still exist at a lower level. Blackwood therefore wants the child to think and mediate his acts; he wants to condition self-control. Thus, for example, the child might utter verbal self-warning statements of the consequences of misbehavior; or he might be asked to write essays on such consequences. That such techniques are workable is also attested by Buys (1972), who points out that reinforcers alter pupils' evaluations of themselves, their behaviors, and their teachers.

But behavior modification is not always used to make changes which some external authority, such as the teacher, deems needed. And it is used not only by behaviorists, but by humanists. The term *behavioral humanism,* seemingly a misnomer, is now being heard. What is meant is that one can use behavior modification techniques, largely reinforcement and punishment, to help people accomplish the changes which they themselves desire — or, put another way, to help them control themselves.

In a clinical setting, one patient came to a therapist complaining of depressing thoughts. A plan was worked out in which she was "allowed" to have depressing thoughts for an hour in the morning and an hour in the afternoon. At other times she was to wear a heavy rubber band around her wrist, and when a depressing thought occurred, to snap it. Her depressing thoughts ceased within three weeks.

Another application of behavior modification is in helping people who wish to lose weight. Thus in one instance a heavyweight was forced to give something he valued to the therapist every week that he had not lost weight. The articles would not be returned until the required weight had been attained. Weight-Watchers of America sometimes use a similar technique, coupled with others such as verbal reinforcement.

Smokers are often helped by behavioral principles. One technique is to use the kind of timer that one carries on a key chain to remind him of time elapsed on a parking meter. He resets this after every cigarette, and does not smoke again until the required time has elapsed. Other devices and techniques include cigarette cases which administer a mild shock or otherwise call attention to the fact that one is smoking, an act which may be so habitual that one is not aware of it.

These techniques are humanist in their applications, in that they are completely voluntary and are frequently self-administered. They are behavioral control in the interest of the individual, who has the freedom to participate or not.

## Conclusion

Events have outcomes. Behavior has consequences. What happens to a person when he behaves in certain ways tends to reinforce or cause him to develop certain attitudes and values as well as the behavior itself. That is why we need to understand operant conditioning. Whether we realize it or not, every human transaction contributes to approach or avoidance behavior and negative or positive feeling tone.

Teaching is aimed at producing learning; hence teachers try to influence pupils. We therefore need to analyze carefully what we do when we are with our students, and to make humane use of operant principles.

Behavior is also learned in other ways. One of the most common is to imitate the actions or opinions of people with whom one identifies. That will be the subject of the next chapter.

SUGGESTIONS FOR FURTHER READING

Ackerman, J. M. *Operant Conditioning Techniques for the Classroom Teacher*. Glenview, Ill.: Scott, Foresman, 1972.

Krumboltz, J. D., and Krumboltz, H. B. *Changing Children's Behavior*. Englewood Cliffs, N.J.: Prentice-Hall, 1972.

MacMillan, D. L. *Behavior Modification in Education*. New York: Macmillan, 1973.

Patterson, C. R., and Gullion, M. E. *Living With Children*. Champaign, Ill.: Research Press, 1968.

Thoresen, C. E., and Mahoney, M. J. *Behavioral Self-control*. New York: Holt, Rinehart, Winston, 1974.

Ulrich, R., Stachnik, T., and Mabry, J. *Control of Human Behavior*. Glenview, Ill.: Scott, Foresman, 1974.

# Chapter 5

## SOCIAL LEARNING AND THE AFFECTIVE DOMAIN

The Student Activist Syndrome . . . *For a while, American newspapers were full of nervous profiles of the nice young boys and girls who went to college and turned bad. Now, a study by two University of Denver psychology professors, reported in the March 18* Washington Evening Star, *has found that student activists are really* extensions of their parents. *Professors John L. Horn and Paul D. Knot found them "generally good students who were imitating their parents and who came from families in which* the father's values were highly respected." *Fathers of activists, according to the findings, tended to be teachers, clergymen, social workers, and other professionals with Ph.D.s. Fathers of hippies — those students who have dropped out of high school and college and who despair of using social machinery for effecting change — tended to be more diverse: businessmen, engineers, airplane pilots, physicians. Parents of activists were atheists, agnostics, Jews, Unitarians, and Friends. Parents of hippies represented a broad cross-section of religious affiliations. Whereas the findings characterized hippies as frequently beset by* parental schism and a strong mother-son relationship, *activists were* "relatively high in self-respect, self-sufficiency, intellectual orientation, and concern for others, *and relatively low in ethnocentrism, possessiveness, and dependency."*

— UNITED STATES CHILDREN'S BUREAU

## The Importance of Social Living

Human beings are not "born human." That is, were an infant to be raised in isolation, or in a nonhuman environment à la Tarzan, we would not expect the developing child to be the same as if he were normally raised. Indeed, accounts of children who have been kept isolated from their parents and other people have shown that such children are unable to communicate adequately; they lack the normal expression of emotions and certain psychomotor skills such as walking; and they seem more primitive in their emotions than normally raised children.

Of course, such accounts can be questioned on the basis that such isolated children may have been born defective, giving parents a reason for hiding them from the public. And the parents themselves may be defective persons. Nevertheless, the fact that isolated children lack words and concepts, many forms of emotional expression, attitudes and values, and social behavior, all lead one to realize the importance of social living. It is necessary, especially during infancy and childhood, to live among others in order to enable us to become "human," especially in the affective domain. This is even true for lower-order animals; Harry and Margaret Harlow have shown that rhesus monkeys raised in isolation from other monkeys do not become adequate adults. The females do not make good mothers; the males are not able to procreate.

## Social Learning Theory

Probably Albert Bandura (Bandura, 1971; Bandura and Walters, 1963) has enunciated social learning theory more clearly than anyone else. Although he recognizes the importance of both classical and operant conditioning, he does not believe that we are as dependent upon the environment as an extreme behavioristic position would indicate. Such a position, although it might be accurate as far as it goes, does not fully explain human behavior. Accordingly additional concepts must be introduced.

Bandura believes that cognitive processes are important because they mediate between stimuli and responses. There is a reciprocal relationship between behavior and the environment in that the environment may stimulate behavior, but cognitive processes interpret the environmental stimuli, determine choice of behavior, and even help determine whether consequences of that behavior are reinforcing or not.

Symbolic processes are similarly influential. We can think through possible courses of action and anticipate the effects of those actions. We can use language to convey ideas, to think with, and to deal with events that are quite distant in time or space.

And we can learn from others quite vicariously. That is, we can observe others and see what happens to them when they behave in certain ways. We model or imitate not only specific behaviors, but more general patterns of behavior (for example, aggression; see Bandura and Walters, 1963). When our models are rewarded for certain acts, they usually show emotion, as they do when they are punished. Not only can we assess how the models are feeling; we may experience some of the same emotion ourselves.

Self-reinforcement, discussed briefly in Chapter 4, is an important part of social learning theory, in that self-reinforcement can be used to explain consistency of behavior. That is, were all reinforcement environmentally administered, we would be at the mercy of a constantly changing environment, and our behavior would swing like a pendulum, depending upon momentary environmental contingencies. If we model ourselves after certain persons, however, we develop our own comparable standards of conduct and reinforce ourselves when we attain those standards. Self-reinforcement can outweigh temporary environmental contingencies.

If we model ourselves after highly competent persons, our own standards are likely to be high and we will reward ourselves only for highly competent behavior. On the other hand, if we have inconsistent models or models who have lower standards, we may ourselves be content with lower levels of behavior, rewarding ourselves accordingly.

Now let us look at the concept of *identifying figures*, the persons or institutions after whom we model ourselves. We have psychologically affiliated ourselves with these persons or institutions in the sense that we have an affinity with them and they have thus become more influential than others in our lives.

We may have many identifying figures. Thus one may be a member of the Jones family, a student at a Midwest university, an American citizen, a Unitarian, and so on. One may identify with some of his friends, his parents, and his teachers. Or he may identify with characters from films, television, or books. In the course of our lives we meet many identifying figures who have varying degrees of influence upon us.

We identify with people for many reasons. One is that in some way we are like them. Thus children tend to identify with others of their age or sex; black people with other black people; athletes with athletes; and so on. This leads to group characteristics and relatively similar attitudes and behaviors among group members. There is a problem, of course, in that individuality may be lost to conformity — one may be stereotyped rather than understood as an individual.

We also identify because the identifying figure reinforces us. Thus we commonly identify with our parents, partly because they provide us with love, attention, and the material necessities.

There is an element of circularity in this. Identifying figures become so partly because they can and do reinforce us; but some reinforcements *are* reinforcements because they are dispensed by identifying figures. Thus one is reinforced more by what his best friends think of him than by what his acquaintances think. And his friends are partly his friends because they usually do think well of him. And because we identify with our professions, we care more about what our colleagues think about our competency than about what someone outside the field might think.

Identification is also influenced by propinquity. Here again, the child identifies with parents, siblings, classmates, and friends partly because he is in closer contact with them. He is influenced by them more frequently, and in turn influences them more.

*Imitation* may be quite deliberate, or it may not be. A neighbor's small son habitually looks at one with raised eyebrows and a quizzical expression so startlingly like that of his dad that it is actually funny; yet it is probably not intentional on the boy's part. But of course the younger children in a family may quite consciously copy the older. Parents frequently remark how quickly younger children develop vocabularies — or for that matter, learn mischievous behaviors.

Models serve us in many ways. They save us time in learning things; each of us need not invent the wheel. They pioneer in problematical situations, so that we can observe their behaviors to see whether they were useful or not. In this way we keep out of a certain amount of trouble. If our model is punished for hitting another child, we vicariously learn that hitting isn't too wise. If the model is rewarded for being polite, the imitator soon learns to be polite also. This is vicarious reinforcement, mentioned earlier.

## Sources for Modelling

Children seem to imitate almost anyone — their parents, friends, characters on TV or in books. We see them playing house, doctor, or even gangster. They also try to eat like Mommy, to dress like their older brothers and sisters, and to ride a bicycle like their friends. They develop attitudes, values, emotional reactions, and other affective characteristics similar to those of their identifying figures. Let's consider some of the major sources for models.

## THE FAMILY

Usually the family is the primary source of identification and modelling and of the subsequent internalization of attitudes and values by the child. Children, after all, receive physical and emotional support from parents. Parents are their initial social contacts in life, and hence they help to determine the direction in which children begin to view themselves and others. Because of the importance of early influences and because of the more extensive dealings parents have with their children, it is not surprising that family influences outweigh those of any other social contacts the child may have. Coleman et al. (1966) have shown that such influences continue throughout the school years and are probably much stronger than anything the school can do to counteract them, should that seem desirable.

All this has importance for the schools. For example, if parents have a negative attitude toward education, the school has a real task in trying to convince the child that education is important to him. A case in point is a certain native American group in which students were urged by the young adults of the group to drop out of high school before graduation. They were taken to task if they tried to be "better than their parents," and sometimes were even beaten or otherwise coerced. On the other hand, in St. Louis County it was found that special efforts to interest the parents of disadvantaged children in the schools and to provide them with books and other educational materials paid off in an improved motivation and achievement on the part of their children.

The quotation introducing this chapter stated that student activists, as compared to hippies, were carrying on the activities and values of their parents. Other research tends to support that hypothesis. Additionally, activists, both protestors and antiprotestors, seem to have much in common. Both groups in Astin's study (1971) differed from randomly selected college students on achievement motivation, dominance, autonomy, exhibition, self-confidence, and aggression. Activists were also more self-accepting. Further, Pierce and Schwartz (1971), who studied picketers in a student strike, found them more welcoming of change and less interested in order, planning, and neatness. Male picketers were more open, friendly, and nondefensive than male nonpicketers; female picketers were more impulsive, heedless of physical safety, interpersonally distant, and fearful of being controlled than nonpicketers. Among both sexes, the college environment was seen as being rich in opportunities for intellectual and interpersonal stimulation, but threatened by administrative arrogance and student passivity. If these students' characteristics may be considered desirable, then Pierce and Schwartz's study has many implications for child-rearing and for making some needed changes in the schools, since it appears to be the families rather than the schools which aid their children in developing these characteristics.

PEERS

As the child reaches school age and especially as he reaches adolescence, the peer group gains in influence over him. It has been suggested that conformity to peer group attitudes may be strongest from age eleven to thirteen. Coleman (1961) showed that although the high schools in his study differed somewhat, in general the "leading crowd" consisted of boys who were athletes and those who were popular with the girls, and that girls preferred to be remembered as activity leaders or as being popular. These findings tie in with the studies of Ringness (1965, 1967), which show that the majority of students desire friendships and affiliation with others more than independence or academic achievement — few wish to think of themselves as nonconformers. These studies imply that the values fostered by the peer group may be different from those of the teachers and may overshadow other adult values.

MISCELLANEOUS MODELS

Other models are provided by the movie screen, television, or literature. Although it can be argued that the attitudes and values of young people have resulted in the popularization of such entertainment groups as the Beatles, along with their hair styles and clothes, it is also true that popular youth idols have greatly influenced the attitudes of their audiences. Songs, films, or readings about protests, sex mores, or drug usage not only reflect the status of the culture, but influence the culture and enhance the likelihood that those people not already committed to certain points of view may become so. Taste in literature may help to dictate what one reads, hence what is published; but on the other hand, what is published helps to dictate what one reads and what opinions he forms.

Controversy concerning the extent of the effects of the media on modelling and behavior has been particularly directed to the question of violence in television programs. Although it is difficult to determine cause and effect, Eron et al. (1972) studied the preference for violent television programs among children in third grade and followed it up ten years later, comparing the preferences to the children's aggressive behaviors. They concluded that watching violent television programs in the early years probably causes actual aggression later. They realized, of course, that television was not the only factor in children's later aggressive behavior. Murray (1973), discussing the Surgeon General's report, feels that there is fairly substantial evidence for at least short-run causation of aggression among some children by violence portrayed on the screen; implications for long-term aggressive behavior are less certain, however. But it does seem clear that it is necessary to do something about violence on the screen. We might infer that showing more desirable behavior on television might have more positive effects on children's behavior, and that censoring alone is not the answer. And certainly teachers should be aware of what is being viewed and be ready to bring pertinent viewings up for class discussion.

CONSISTENCY AMONG MODELS

We might expect that the child, influenced by his parents, would associate with peers from homes with like attitudes and values, and would therefore internalize those values. To some extent that is true, at least for school achievement motivation (Ringness, 1970). The child rarely finds complete consistency among the attitudes of his various identifying figures, however, especially when he reaches adolescence and becomes more mobile.

Of course, in closed societies, such as the Amish community, where there is relatively little contact with outside society and where everyone reinforces certain ways of life, the child ordinarily accepts the prevailing values; such societies usually change relatively little from one generation to another. In the case of the Amish, clothing styles, hair length, beards, and the use of the horse and buggy endure. So, too, do attitudes toward schooling, economic self-sufficiency, and obedience to the law.

On the other hand, you, as a student, have been exposed to and have felt the pressures of various groups' life styles and philosophies. Your present beliefs may be very different from those you held on entering the university.

In essence, if parents, peers, teachers, and the media all portray

common values, the child may well accept them for his own. But if there is conflict among the values held by various identifying figures, he is caught. He may accept the values of those with whom he most identifies; he may accept a few values from some figures and a few from others, or he may make some sort of compromise. Unfortunately, there is a fourth alternative: he may simply become confused and form no stable values of his own.

Attitudes and values learned through identification and imitation may be adopted quite uncritically, and in that sense are not really one's own so much as carbon copies of someone else's. But, with maturation, especially in adolescence and early adulthood, the young person is inclined to reexamine his beliefs and ask himself such questions as "Who am I?" "What do I really believe?" "Where am I going?" This is a time when one goes beyond simple modelling and restructures for himself, internalizing his value system. One may still search for models and heroes, but the process is complicated. He may reject earlier notions of what he would like to be, on the grounds that he had never realized the implications of his earlier views, but had simply adopted them. Or he may find such views confirmed. This is part of the process of education, and it is up to the schools as well as the home to provide suitable identifying figures, both alive and in the literature, and thus to help youth explore the implications of various values, rather than to leave the learning process to chance.

## Negative Identification

The term negative identification is used to indicate rejection of certain persons or institutions, together with their behaviors, attitudes, and values. One reason for negative identification is that the child himself has been rejected by the identifying figures, or has had little reinforcement from them.

Think of the number of times a school fails to reward students for positive effort; instead, every dereliction or inadequacy is noted. We considered earlier a high school in which the truants were suspended if absent too often. One wonders how that procedure would reinforce the attitude that school is valuable and studying a useful thing to do. Other examples might be the competitive grading system, which tends to ensure that only a few students will attain high marks. Again, consider the connotations of having to get permission to go to the bathroom or to get a drink of water.

### A CASE STUDY

A study was made in a midwestern city in which high-school-age young people were found to be milling around town on week nights as well as on weekends. They did not seem to have any particular purpose, nor did they form cohesive groups, although in the aggregate there were several hundred such youth. Some were nuisances, and some were delinquent. Adults were pushed off the sidewalk, coffee shops were invaded and the furniture abused, ice balls were thrown at passing cars, theaters were crashed, and so on.

A young social worker was able to gain sufficient acceptance among some of these youth to question them. He found that when he asked them who won the basketball game that night, a typical answer was "I don't know. Who's playing?" The majority of the youth did not identify with their high schools. Some had dropped out and others were in the process.

A check among teachers and student leaders showed some of the reasons for lack of school identification. For one thing, the street corner youth were not accepted by the faculty. Frequently they were stereotyped as coming from the "——— part of town, and you know what that makes him," or as being unclean and poorly dressed, or from a home where the parents were "no better than they should be." Such youth were seen as discipline problems, poor learners, lazy, and otherwise a thorn in teachers' sides. Teacher behaviors included sarcasm, humiliation, and punishment, but only rarely was acceptance shown — and that depended upon whether the youth had particular abilities, such as athletic prowess. Worse, the youth were not accepted by the majority of students. They were ignored, excluded from clubs, avoided because of "bad reputations," and so on.

Street corner behavior, then, was partly an attempt to find others with whom one could affiliate. Being rejected by the majority, street corner youth in turn rejected more conventional peer and adult values, and reinforced each other in deviant behaviors. It is not surprising that some·youth, originally relatively harmless, eventually turned to auto theft, the use of hard drugs, burglary, and mugging.

Many fairly typical school practices are not only inefficient but inhumane. For example, it is not uncommon to lump the "problem kids" together under a "strong" teacher. Those students, knowing why they are isolated, tend to regard the school as a prison, and their goals become giving the teacher a hard time, escaping work, and marking time until they can drop out. Some become quite hardened and are heard from via vandalism, brutality to other students, or bomb threats.

Similar phenomena can be found in almost any university. Some students have acted violently, dressed extremely, or joined the drug culture. Such students may be identifying with each other as dropouts from the larger society. Sometimes they genuinely feel that society has failed them, and say there is too much hypocrisy and emphasis on material values. Since "the system" cannot be changed, and since they feel they cannot work within the system, they avoid the larger culture. But for others this attitude represents rationalization, used to cover the fact that they have not gained acceptance by more successful sudents.

## Learning and Performance

The question arises as to what one learns from observing models. Does he learn a novel activity? Does he change an attitude? If his behavior changes after observing a model, what may be the reasons?

Bandura and Walters (1963) performed a number of experiments in which a model was shown hitting, kicking, and otherwise abusing a Bobo doll (an inflated, clownlike doll). They found two results among the small children who were observers. One was that the children learned novel behaviors shown by the model, although they did not always use them; whether or not they did was controlled somewhat by whether the model was shown to be reinforced for his behavior. But there was also a "disinhibiting effect," in which children who observed the model being reinforced for aggressive behavior toward the doll were much more inclined to be aggressive themselves when given a Bobo doll to play with. A similar effect is said to have been observed by a psychologist studying the effect of Sunday professional football on husbands who watched habitually. The husbands were said to have become more "aggressive" to their wives after a hard-fought game than on days when no game took place.

Earlier, we discussed the fact that attitudes and values are not always reflected in overt behavior (p. 30). We observed that there were situational variables to consider, as well as the fact that each of us has a hierarchy of values and that in certain situations some take precedence over others. Thus in the school situation a child may have a very real desire to do well in his studies, yet may be afraid to show too much effort because of pressures from his peer group. Again, a boy may fear that he will be called a sissy if he plays with small children, even though he may wish to do so very much.

We therefore find that we have to decide whether or not someone has learned a value but is not able to carry it into action, or whether he has not learned it at all. This is not easy, and sometimes it is impossible to tell; but it may be worth the effort of trying to find out by further observation, conversation with the person, or even discussion with parents or others who might know.

## Some Implications for the Schools

In my own research I have been interested in the achievement values of pupils and the relationships of such values to achievement over, at, or under expectation (Ringness, 1970). In a referrant study of mine eighth-grade girls were asked to respond to an attitude scale which provided information about the degree to which they identified with father, mother, and best friends and teachers, and about the school achievement values they attributed to those figures and to themselves. It was found that the identification and achievement values of the identifying figures were indeed related to the achievement values of the girls, and the girls' values, in turn, to actual achievement. On the whole, the girls felt that both parents had quite high achievement values for their daughters; it was the degree of identification with the parents that differentiated over, under, and average achievement.

On the other hand, the girls identified strongly with their best friends, as expected, and it was the strength of achievement values of the friends which differentiated among the achievers. In the aggregate, girls tended to be "best friends" with girls who held similar values.

Both the degree of identification with and the achievement values attributed to teachers were less than for parents. The fact that teachers are not as strong identifying figures is not too surprising. After all, parents have both more extended and earlier relationships with their children than do teachers; teachers see more children, and for fewer hours per day; the range of activities involving teachers with children is more limited; and parents and peers have more reinforcements to offer. But the finding that teachers are not seen as being greatly concerned with getting children to achieve is significant; it may be that the teachers were really more concerned with "telling" than with motivating.

HOW TEACHERS CAN IMPROVE IDENTIFICATION
AND MODELLING

People tend to identify with others who identify with them. Teachers need to identify with their pupils. This means having concern for each boy and girl in the class. It does not mean getting chummy or prying into children's private lives.

The excellent teacher will try to accept each child, be interested in him, and have confidence in him; and he should enjoy working with children. Studies have shown (e.g., Ringness, 1952) that the motives for teaching of successful elementary teachers center on concern, first for the child and second for the subject matter. For secondary teachers the order is reversed. A third motive, that of job satisfaction as measured by salary, working hours, vacations, and other "practical" benefits of the profession, is characteristic of the motives of less successful teachers at both levels.

If teachers are really concerned about pupils and identified with them, how should they show their concern? Most of us can think of a few teachers who were willing to spend extra time with us, who spoke to us on the street, who noticed if we were not feeling well, who listened to our ideas, who were willing to admit pupils' points in arguments, and who tried to develop their policies with the students' points of view in mind.

But notice how few teachers sit with students in the school cafeteria or at a basketball game. How few remark when an absentee returns after an illness, and how few take students with them on trips to out-of-town school events. But experience will show that even mild attempts to involve oneself informally with the students will produce responsiveness.

Teachers can reinforce students more than they do. This point needs no further elaboration. But consider not only reinforcing for creative, attentive, and problem-solving behaviors, but also for less formal behaviors, in the classroom or anywhere else. Do you remember a teacher who noticed the school newspaper's account of your summer vacation trip or your scoring at the last football game? Or one who thought the dress you made was most attractive? Or one who was aware that you had spent considerable time tutoring for a preschool enrichment program?

Students identify with and model themselves after successful persons. Teachers are viewed as people as well as professionals. It is essential that they be perceived as successful people in the sense of having well-adjusted personalities and good social relationships; they must in all ways be admirable as persons, regardless of status or financial position. Those who seem to be cheerful and confident, to enjoy their work, and to be motivated to teach are more likely to be chosen as models than those who seem frustrated, tired, fearful, or unhappy. Furthermore, teachers who really know their material, who are businesslike, and who expect students to learn are better identifying figures than those who are slipshod, unorganized, lazy, permissive, or who "play to the gallery."

Obviously, not all teachers can be identifying figures for all pupils. For example, boys may find it difficult to model after a female teacher. They may not wish to model after one who appears too goody-goody. Or they may reject a teacher because of his ethnic origins or his status in the community. This is unfortunate, for such teachers may be excellent examples of human living and professional conduct.

Yet every teacher will have *some* pupils with whom he has a relatively close relationship. This is not only natural, but is good, so long as he does not make favorites of them. The athletic coach, English teacher, bandmaster — indeed, all teachers — can be identifying figures for students interested in their subjects. They can even become counsellors as well as models.

The kind of moral model the teacher portrays is important. We do not need teachers with detrimental attitudes or values. This is especially true if the teacher has considerable charisma, for children have less experience on which to make their judgments than do adults; hence they are more easily influenced. Certainly teachers who are immoral, hypocritical, or mentally ill, or who lead children into undesirable conduct, should not be in the classroom. Unfortunately, there are more such teachers than one usually realizes. Kaplan (1959) claimed that as many as three million children each day spend their time with teachers too emotionally ill to be teaching.

Of course, the terms *immoral*, *hypocritical*, and *mentally ill* are value-laden words. Thus, although most of us would agree that we don't want teachers in the classroom under the influence of alcohol or drugs, we may differ as to other characteristics. For example, we may very well feel that teachers who can see some of the drawbacks of our present society and are therefore considered activists should be employed.

## OTHER IMPLICATIONS

What about models other than teachers? Continuing with achievement motivation as an example, can the school do it all? We would like children to be reasonably convinced that school tasks are worth doing and that successful accomplishment is in their best interest now and in the future. We would like to have children find value in their work. (Debate on this point is irrelevant: if school tasks are not useful, the curriculum should be changed; we should not simply allow unmotivated students to put in their time.)

Since we know that children identify with parents and peers and are influenced by their achievement values, it would seem that to help the child develop achievement values one would want to go beyond simply working with him as an individual. We might want to work with other identifying figures so that collective influences could be brought to bear to help the child internalize the value of school achievement. Several methods suggest themselves.

For example, attempts might be made to improve the achievement orientation of the entire student body, or at least the members of the immediate classroom. This might be done through discussions, incentives, academic competition with other rooms or schools, awards, job counselling, science fairs, and so on.

We might also consider the advantages of providing good achievement models for the poorer students. This would call for the end of the tracking system, at least in part. We could plan for better students to mingle with and perhaps help the poorer, possibly even acting as junior-level teaching assistants. This would also call for recognition of whatever abilities *any* pupil has, so that they might be used for the good of all. For example, Niles was a poor student but was good at catching snakes, frogs, and other small animals. He eventually became curator of the biology laboratory. Lloyd, an average student, was nevertheless a leader in the cornet section of the band and eventually became the student conductor. In both instances the boys' own motivation and achievement improved, partly because their abilities were recognized.

*Parents* should be worked with much more than usual. Furthermore, when parent conferences are held, Dad should definitely be involved. Our data (Ringness, 1965, 1970) show that the fathers' values seem to influence school achievement a bit more than those of the mothers, especially with boys. This is backed by the experience of some school psychologists, who find more healthy changes occurring when they have conferences with the father or with both parents rather than with the mother alone. One reason for this may be that the American father has traditionally played a rather passive role in the child's upbringing. After consultation he is more likely to reinforce the mother's efforts, perhaps tipping the scales toward success. (It is obviously easier for a child to follow a model if both parents project the same one.) Or the mother may not be as achievement-oriented as the father, who may be working in the competitive business world. Again, the poorly achieving boy may simply need a male model.

Schools ought to be concerned also with models on television and in books, drama, and movies, and music. Allport (1961) feels that these sources tend to induce strong identification, and thus are influential in building values. In addition to knowing what the child experiences in the media, teachers can use such sources in classroom activities.

Achievement motivation is not the only value influenced by social learning, but we have used it as one example of how schools might be concerned with identification and modelling. The same principles apply to other attitudes and values.

## Conclusion

Identification and imitation may be purposeful or not. In any case, the child models himself after many identifying figures. Sometimes the models do not fit our notions of what models should be. Sometimes there is conflict among them. We need to recognize the models to which children are exposed, employ them as constructively as possible, and try to provide positive identifying figures of our own.

Using Kohlberg's table of moral development (pages 28–29), we can relate his work to the material in Chapters 4 through 6. Although at this point we can only speculate, the Preconventional Level, Stages 1 and 2, seem oriented toward avoidance of punishment and attainment of reward. One might think of those stages as being governed by operant principles. The Conventional Level, Stages 3 and 4, seem more oriented toward identification, as Kohlberg says. But in the Post-Conventional Level, Stages 5 and 6, it would appear that one needs to go beyond reward, punishment, and identification. This might require "cognitive restructuring" of some kind, or the application of humanistic techniques; indeed, Kohlberg's techniques of moving up from one level to another do involve rethinking of one's values, as we will see in Chapter 8.

Our next chapter deals with cognitive restructuring. Although conditioning and imitation are involved, we will see an emphasis on cognition as a factor in the acquisition and application of attitudes, values, and other affective behavior.

## SUGGESTIONS FOR FURTHER READING

Bandura, A. "Social Learning Theory of Identificatory Processes," in Goslin, D. A. (ed.), *Handbook of Socialization Theory and Research.* Chicago: Rand-McNally, 1969, pp. 213–62.

Bandura, A. *Social Learning Theory.* Morristown, N.J.: General Learning Press, 1971.

Bandura, A., and Walters, R. H. *Adolescent Aggression.* New York: Ronald Press, 1959.

Ringness, T. A. *Mental Health in the Schools.* New York: Random House, 1968, Chapters 2, 5.

# Chapter 6

---

# COGNITIVE RESTRUCTURING
# AND AFFECTIVE BEHAVIOR

*. . . The most common means of teaching values employed by teachers in the past has been that of moralistic* telling. *Teachers have used a variety of hortatory and persuasive techniques, emotional pleas, appeals to conscience, slogans, and "good examples" to help students learn to value the "right" objects, persons, or ideas. A corollary of moralism is the argument for "exposure." According to this argument, the way to help students acquire certain desired values is to expose them continually to the kinds of objects and ideas which possess such values (e.g., a painting by Renoir, a Mozart sonata,* Caesar's Commentaries — *in Latin, of course). In short, if we provide the "right" kind of atmosphere in our classrooms, our students will "catch" the values we desire them to possess. Our job as teachers, then, is to assure that we place our students in the kinds of situations and expose them to the kinds of materials that contain the kinds of values we want "caught." (Should any student not catch these values, naturally something must be wrong with the student!)*

*The problem with these approaches is that they just haven't worked very well. "If admonition, lecture, sermon, or example were fully effective instruments in gaining compliance with codes of conduct, we would have reformed long ago the criminal, the delinquent, or the sinner." The sad fact is that exhortation rarely produces committed, actively involved individuals. Essentially, it involves one-way communication, yet several studies have indicated that one-directional, persuasive communications are relatively ineffective.*

— J. R. FRAENKEL

Is Fraenkel correct? Or is he partially correct? Does persuasion never work? If it does, under what conditions? What cognitive factors affect attitude formation and change? We must consider these questions.

At this point we will not ask whether one should attempt to teach certain values or not; neither will we ask which values one should teach, if he should attempt to do so. These are philosophical and political questions which the reader must answer as he sees fit, but we should realize that whether we know it or not, each of us portrays and perhaps unconsciously tries to inculcate a value system.

Since we are all subjected to attempts to create in us certain values or value changes, then, and since some of us may indeed wish to inculcate certain values in our pupils, some study of cognitive methods is needed.

This chapter deals with *cognitive restructuring*, a term that refers to both the initial learning of interests, attitudes, and values and to the modification of present affective states. Cognitive learning implies thought processes which might involve reception, discrimination, perception, projection of consequences, problem-solving, evaluating, and decision-making. Thus cognitive restructuring is different from conditioning or imitation because it demands intellectual processing of data.

To illustrate, at some time in your life you probably did not particularly understand or value democracy. But during childhood and your school years you may have learned to value it. Furthermore, at one time you may have valued democracy highly, yet your experiences may have caused you to rethink your position and come up with the idea of consensus as opposed to majority rule. In other words, you may have evaluated the idea of democracy and experienced a value change.

Attitudes and values become cognitively structured in several ways. We shall be dealing here with indoctrination, persuasion, and cognitive dissonance. Later chapters will deal with other (humanistic) techniques.

## Indoctrination

Indoctrination refers to the direct teaching of attitudes and values to someone, often a child. In this method a given point of view is repeatedly stressed and the recipient is urged to adopt it as his own. Usually other points of view are not considered, or if considered, are described as wrong, distasteful, stupid, or heretical. In indoctrination the learner has limited choices. He must either accept or reject the attitude being pressed upon him. If he rejects the official position, he may find himself ostracized or otherwise in difficulties with the institution that is attempting to indoctrinate him.

The success of indoctrination depends upon the extent to which a closed society, in which all members reinforce the same values, can be developed. Such societies do exist — for instance, certain religious colonies — and their members are protected from outside influences wherever possible. The Amish, mentioned in Chapter 5, not only foster particular hair styles, clothing, and the use of horse-drawn vehicles, but also a particular value system. They educate their children in their own schools and resist influences from the broader American society toward altering or extending their curricula.

The members of this cultural group have considerable security, and their roles are well-defined. There is little or no reason to question the teachings of the family, church, and school. There are real advantages to accepting community values; conflicts exist only when such a community must interact with the broader culture and either win acceptance for its position or capitulate. A case in point is the conflict over whether the Amish must conform to a state law concerning the age at which children may leave school, and whether the children must attend public high school.

Another example is that seen in underdeveloped countries such as Ethiopia. In the rural areas of these nations there is a long tradition in which males are considered important and females more or less their chattels. Public education has been resisted, and sex roles have been cherished. As a result, few women have been educated, and a medieval way of life has been perpetuated. This has been possible because many communities have been isolated from the more progressive urban areas, and it has been in the interests of the priests, nobles, and landowners to foster a static way of life. The central government is striving hard to promote education, which is likely to challenge older attitudes and values.

A less happy form of indoctrination was seen in Nazi Germany, where book-burnings were common, dissenters were tortured or killed, and the press and other media were completely controlled. In such a repressive society, those who do raise questions are soon disposed of.

Russia and the People's Republic of China employ indoctrination today. So, too, does the United States, although in a less obtrusive form. In the former countries the schoolroom is used to produce loyal communists as well as for teaching subject matter. Community meetings, billboards, radio, the press, and other media all stress the party line. In the United States we claim to be liberal and oriented toward individual and cultural differences. Yet in some communities there have been attempts at censoring the books in libraries and schools. Thus some of the works of Malcolm X and Eldridge Cleaver and some books about sex education have been removed from shelves where adolescents might choose them. Again, there is controversy over pornography, and bookstores and theaters have been closed. This sort of censorship is an attempt at indoctrination by withholding ideas from people. As we know, it has not been very successful, because too many people differ on such values.

SOME CONCERNS

Indoctrination works best with small children and with people who are relatively uneducated. Children, because they depend upon adults and have learned to trust them, and because they lack experience, usually accept adults' views without much questioning. They are regularly reinforced for expressing certain beliefs. Probably your own basic attitudes were learned at an early age as a result of indoctrination as well as by modelling and reinforcement. You will recognize honesty, cleanliness, doing one's best, and competitive striving as the kind of values that middle-class parents stress to their children many times each week; and the children are urged not to question such teachings. It is "Do as I say and never mind why" in many homes.

One problem with indoctrination is that it does not really allow children to think through alternatives to the attitudes and values presented to them; ideas are promoted in such ways that children must accept them quite without question. As the child matures and enters a broader environment in which alternatives may prevail, he may at first cling blindly to the attitudes with which he was indoctrinated; but later he may be susceptible to change, since he really had not made the original attitudinal decisions for himself. The finding that others have different beliefs from oneself and that those beliefs may be legitimate can produce some emotional upset. Some children may then reject parental teachings; others may isolate themselves from the new group; still others may be confused.

We should not overlook the fact that indoctrination may contribute to prejudice against those who do not believe as we do. In brief, if we think we are correct and others are wrong, we tend to look down upon them and to isolate ourselves from them. We may become blindly prejudiced against them and afraid to open ourselves up to real communication with them. You are doubtless familiar with the irrational fear of communism, the inability to communicate with members of minority cultures, and the negative feelings about people with strongly different religious or political convictions evidenced by a great many Americans.

It is true that society is the source of most of our need satisfactions. Certain ways of life must therefore be promoted if society is to survive; hence the dominant values must be fostered at an early age. From this point of view, indoctrination is legitimate. Thus parents teach children fundamental values, such as respect for laws and mores, because otherwise not only society but the children themselves might suffer. It is also true that the young need structure in their lives, because immaturity, lack of knowledge, and lack of judgment might prevent them from making reasonable value choices. The too permissive or ambiguous parent may do more harm than good, leaving his children confused, in conflict, or insecure because they have nothing to hold on to.

It may be argued that indoctrination is wrong because society needs many changes. It is inescapably true that we need change. But indoctrination never succeeds completely. It does not cover all aspects of social living, and it varies somewhat from family to family and from community to community. And there are always enough differences of opinion so that changes do come about.

Furthermore, putting a complete stop to indoctrination would probably be as bad as too much indoctrination. Healthy change is usually gradual and does not represent a complete upheaval and discard of all previous attitudes and values. When changes are too sweeping, the usual result is first a period of confusion and perhaps even anarchy, but eventually a repressive new society in which the original values are replaced by a new set of values which is rigidly indoctrinated and enforced — witness the French, Russian, Chinese, and Nazi revolutions.

The question then becomes one of when to try to indoctrinate and when not. The answer affects school practices, for schools really do try to indoctrinate children. For example, we typically foster democracy, the idea that education is important, and the belief that if one tries hard he will succeed. Our efforts bear varying degrees of success. As agents of society we do indeed have certain obligations to preserve that society, but we would also like to see certain aspects of society improved. The difficulty is that we therefore must promote some values, yet at the same time try to educate so that intelligent choices can be made.

Any efforts to indoctrinate will be more likely to succeed if the value of our teachings can be seen and tested by the children. For instance, schools have lost credibility among the young by mishandling drug education. We have tried to promote a moralistic viewpoint and to scare children into avoiding drugs, yet they may know more of the truth about drugs than do their teachers. Again, the deprived have lost faith in the values of education for upward social mobility; in our society it has not paid off well for them. Instances such as these tend to alienate children and youth, and that alienation affects schoolwork in general. We need to deal with values that can be legitimately substantiated rather than with notions based on bias or inadequate knowledge.

## Persuasive Communication

Have you ever purchased a set of encyclopedias you really did not want? Have you paid more for an automobile than you had planned because it had prestigious features? Have you ever experienced religious conversion in response to the pleas of an eloquent evangelist? Have you ever rapped with someone about an attitude or value and changed your own position?

In many, if not most, interpersonal transactions, someone is trying to persuade someone else that there is something he should do, think, or become. Teachers use this technique in "motivating" pupils to attempt to learn. We are using persuasion when we try to convince a child that he should not drop out of school, or urge him to become more orderly, or talk to the class about ethics. In addition to trying to induce behavior change, we are trying to inculcate values.

Persuasion is usually conceived of by the teacher as a means of getting the pupil to do something for his own good; however, it is also for the teacher's good, a point that is frequently overlooked. It becomes essential to ask ourselves, Is this really in the pupil's best interests, or am I simply trying to impose my values on him?

When we persuade we use a variety of techniques. We present information to bolster our arguments; we appeal to the emotions; we exercise charisma; and we promise reinforcement. The advertising business is particularly good at persuasion. We are caused to embrace all manner of beliefs ("All aspirin is *not* alike"), and our values are manipulated. Witness the worship of youth, the appeal to hedonism, the desire for prestige or power. Notice also how politicians proceed. They seek out issues, sometimes false, and try to persuade us to embrace their points of view. Thus we have cries of alarm, promises upon promises, and dramatic denunciations. And of course politicians create favorable public images for themselves, which may or may not represent their true nature.

What factors in persuasive activity influence the results? After all, if we *are* going to try to persuade, we might as well try to maximize our chances for success.

## PREDISPOSITIONS OF THE LEARNER

Consider questions on which many people hold opposing points of view: Should there be sex education in the schools? Shall we legalize marijuana? Should children be bussed to force integration in the schools? Many of us have firm convictions on these issues, based on what we consider appropriate evidence. We therefore may try to persuade others of their correctness. (Whether we should do so is another question.)

Our best tactics are to be as honest and open-minded as possible in our presentations, showing that we recognize the opposition and that our opponents may have valid arguments. We should present as many sides to the question as we can, mustering the arguments, summing up in favor of our position. If we cannot logically do this, we may decide to change our own position on the issue. (On the other hand, if most of the persons to be convinced are already somewhat favorably inclined, we might do well to stress the positive aspects of the position we take and try not to introduce unfavorable arguments.)

Take the high school geometry class as an example. Many of the students probably do not like mathematics, but must take geometry because it is required. They may have a variety of reasons for disliking it, but usually their reasons include fear of not doing well, anticipation of difficult and boring assignments, and failure to see the relevance of geometry to their lives. These predispositions probably have root in past personal experiences, although they may simply be traditional among the student group.

The teacher might discuss why geometry could have negative connotations. He should recognize the validity of the arguments, countering them when possible, but also face the fact that some arguments cannot be countered. In the latter event he would try to show that the advantages of studying geometry outweigh the disadvantages.

The teacher might show that geometry is somewhat different from algebra or arithmetic. He could show that his own attitude toward students is supportive, and that he would test and mark in ways that should maximize the probability of success and minimize anxiety. He might admit that some of the work is dull or arduous, but that it will not last forever and will lead to future attainment and satisfaction. He could try to relate geometry to the everyday lives of the students. For example, students who enjoy art might make use of geometry in sculpture; those scientifically inclined might find uses for vectors; others might be interested in architecture, automobile design, or even sailing. Or geometry might be introduced as a form of logic, comparable to syllogisms and extended argument. The teacher might stress its problem-solving aspects, presenting it as a puzzle and stressing the thought process rather than the outcome.

In brief, the teacher should present both the advantages and the disadvantages as honestly as possible. After all, some students might take pride in rising to the challenges of a rigorous subject. Of course, if the students are already favorably disposed, the teacher need only encourage them in order to keep them interested.

PERSONAL INVOLVEMENT

We usually participate more in discussions when we feel that an issue is important to us. Such concern may either work to the advantage of or inhibit attitude change.

If our own lives are threatened in any way, our personal involvement may simply raise defenses. Thus it is easy to accept minority group members if we rarely encounter them and if they pose no economic competition or other threat to us; but those of us who frequently interact with other cultural groups are likely to form strong opinions for or against them, depending upon the positive or negative experiences we have had in such encounters. Integration of schools, for instance, may contribute to successful interaction between ethnic groups, but it sometimes produces polarization.

On the other hand, without personal involvement, attitude change is less likely to occur. If we see an opportunity for self-enhancement by changing some of our attitudes, the more involved we are, the better the chance of such change.

PRINCIPLES OF PERSUASIVE COMMUNICATION

Both classical and operant conditioning are related to the power of persuasive communication. Recall that words have both denotative and connotative meanings — that is, they convey certain concepts, but they also carry particular meanings and feelings which depend upon the previous learning of the individual. Classical conditioning is of interest to us here, since words carry emotional tones. For example, how do you feel when the words *fiancée, Christmas,* or *peace* are presented to you? How do you feel about *sweat, war,* or *vomit?*

Quite obviously the persuader should employ as many words with positive connotations as possible, and he should avoid the negative. Thus politicians are said to be fond of such phrases as *mother, home, country,* and even *apple pie.* Of course, to arouse emotions and get people angry enough to take radical action, our more explosive writers, such as Jerry Rubin, are fond of words such as *pig, mother-f———,* and the like.

Operant conditioning comes in when the persuader uses positive reinforcement or the promise of such reinforcement. We see this in advertising when we are told we will better our mileage with a certain brand of tire or are promised a set of steak knives if we open a savings account at a particular bank. In school we as persuaders may proclaim the advantages of study by trying to show that more education produces entree to better jobs and higher income, that certain courses of study lead to more enjoyment of life, or that study will bring good grades.

Threat or expectation of punishment tends to produce resistance to persuasion. Few of us are "saved" by fear of damnation. Schools oriented toward punishment for transgressions do not commonly produce favorable attitudes toward school. For example, when detention is used for failure to complete schoolwork, the school is implying that studying is an unpleasant task, and pupils may direct their efforts to avoiding punishment rather than achieving. Consider all the motivations to cheat, to purchase a term paper from a commercial source, to plagiarize, or to steal examination copies in advance when failure is used to try to persuade students to study.

### PERSONALITY OF THE COMMUNICATOR

Advertisers know the value of training salesmen to improve their personalities. We are more prone to listen to the friendly, outgoing person who appears to have our interests at heart. The insurance salesman makes every effort to make you feel comfortable, to have you believe that he likes and respects you, to be entertaining and humorous, and to listen to your ideas. He is careful in dress and language and molds himself to your tastes in companions. In other words, he tries to be someone you can identify with. Sales managers choose different personalities to work with different people and products. The Cadillac salesman is quite different from the used car salesman. The man who deals with farmers is likely to be quite different from the man who purveys stocks and bonds to the wealthy. Similarly, notice the differences in the advertising aimed at different readers — for example, the ads in *Playboy, Sports Afield,* and the *Wall Street Journal* are quite unlike each other.

Aronson (1969) has addressed himself to some of the "antecedents" of interpersonal attraction involved in persuasion. Among others, he considers propinquity — that is, the fact that we are attracted more to relatives and neighbors than to strangers ("Bank at your friendly *neighborhood* bank"). Other antecedents include similarity of beliefs and values, similarity of personal traits, and complementary need systems. Thus interpersonal attraction can be understood from a social learning model: we are likely to be mutually attractive when we view each other as persons of high ability and find each other to have pleasant or agreeable characteristics or behavior — in other words, we like people who like us. All of this contributes to mutual reward or reinforcement.

In the schools some teachers are more influential with pupils than others. A teacher who seems aloof, unfriendly, dowdy, or in any way unsuccessful or colorless will be less likely to influence pupil opinion than the confident, open, "involved" teacher. Many studies have shown that the personality characteristics of teachers (cf. Ringness, 1968), such as sense of humor, liking for children, openness to encounter with pupils, and enthusiasm, count most when students are asked to evaluate a course or a teacher.

The prestige of the communicator is also important. Bem (1970) points out that in any group some persons tend to be sought for their opinions on specific things, and thereby influence the actions of the seekers. Prestige, in this instance, does not mean high social or professional status so much as it means expertise, soundness of judgment, trustworthiness, and so on. Thus any of us might be sought out for our thinking on a subject in which we are known to have expertise, but few of us would be influential in general.

Quite obviously teachers need to develop their competency in their specific fields. Students are more willing to accept ideas from teachers who can demonstrate excellence in their subjects. Thus the music teacher should be a skilled performer; the teacher of science might well have some industrial or research experience; the coach should have a reputation as an outstanding former player. And for the same reason, one should probably refrain from teaching out of his field.

## Cognitive Dissonance

Leon Festinger (1964) has publicized cognitive dissonance perhaps more than most writers. He makes the point that sometimes a person finds himself in a position where he is acting, or is forced to act, in ways contrary to his real feelings or attitudes. In that event he takes steps to bring his attitudes and his actions into greater congruence —

that is, to reduce the dissonance between his feelings and his actions. This can be done by revising one's attitudes or values; altering one's behavior; or using defense mechanisms such as rationalization, projection, or denial of reality.

A decade ago I studied bright ninth-grade boys who were achieving poorly in school (Ringness, 1963). When faced with the fact that their abilities and stated desires to do well did not square with their poor grades, they made a number of interesting statements. Some boys simply blamed teachers for being unfair in grading. Others mentioned that their classmates cheated, but that they themselves would not stoop to such practices. Others said they were aware of the dissonance and were actively trying to study harder. Some denied that they were bright. Others noted that perhaps they really didn't value education that much, after all. But all of them took steps of one kind or another to reduce the obvious dissonance between their stated achievement values and their actual performance.

This sort of thing was also seen at a university when the faculty were caught between the need to support policies imposed by legislation and administration and their own agreement with students who opposed those policies. The grading system, smoking in the classroom, protests and demonstrations, course requirements, and strikes by teaching assistants all produced dissonant situations. The teaching assistants' strike was called for better pay, lower workloads, tenure, and health benefits. Some of the faculty saw legitimacy in the demands of the assistants, but felt that as professors they should continue to hold classes and carry out other professional duties. Their formerly favorable attitudes toward the assistants and their demands tended to become less favorable during the strike. Other members of the staff continued to see value in the assistants' demands, and accordingly stopped holding classes and did not check to see whether the assistants were on duty or not.

In cognitive dissonance there are three principles that need to be considered:

1. Dissonance creates a motivational effect to reduce such dissonance.
2. One tends to resist new information if it will create new dissonance. (For example, a bright student might resist someone's pointing out to him how able he really is.)
3. If new information seems likely to reduce the dissonance, it will be sought. (For example, if one must study a subject which he deems valueless, he may welcome any evidence that shows it to be relevant. Unfortunately, he might instead be reinforced in his

original attitude by complaints made by others, and end up studying less — or even dropping the subject.)

In dealing with cognitive dissonance, one wants to be sure that the learner is not simply escaping his dilemma through rationalizing. For example, a teacher might find himself trying to be affable to pupils whom he really does not like. A form of rationalizing might be "These lower-class kids need the example and influence of someone like me so they will have a chance to improve themselves." This does not reduce the dissonance, but masks it. Furthermore, it is ineffective; such a teacher is likely to be viewed as a phony. The teacher should rearrange his values, or if he cannot, he should refrain from the masquerade.

In dealing with dissonance one must first try to find ways to demonstrate that dissonance in as nonthreatening a manner as possible. He can help the learner to understand the alternatives to his present ways of behaving and to his attitudes and values. New information can be presented, and the learner can be asked to reconsider both his attitudes and behavior. Some form of counselling rather than direct teaching may work best.

BEM'S POSITION

Daryl Bem (1970) offers a counter-theory to explain the fact that attitudes are frequently altered following contradictory overt behavior. The cognitive dissonance theory is that one changes his attitudes to coincide with his behavior, but Bem believes that one may not really hold attitudes very strongly, or that they may not be consciously recognized. Thus when a person engages in a behavior, he *convinces* himself of his attitudes. In a way, he says to himself, "Since I am engaging in this sort of act, it must be that I believe in it." Bem's contention is that attitudes follow behavior without much thought on a person's part. Of course, once developed and recognized, attitudes naturally help to direct future behavior.

The overall import of Bem's position is quite similar to that of the cognitive dissonance theory — namely, when a person is involved in acts which reflect attitudes or values others think are desirable, he is likely to adopt those attitudes.

## Prejudice

In one of our classes a graduate student related an incident concerning a professor at another university who proposed not to allow a certain doctoral candidate to attain his degree, not because he was an incompetent scholar, but because he was a racist. The professor felt that such a person would be a bad influence on his students. Discussion ranged through such questions as whether one could ethically withhold a degree because of the candidate's attitudes, whether the professor himself was not forcing a value system upon his candidates, whether the student should have been screened out earlier or even denied admission, whether counselling should have been instituted, and how affective learning should relate to the doctoral degree. Not only are these complicated questions, capable of almost endless debate, but it is clear that issues such as these are hot ones and that there is considerable concern over evidence of racism in prospective teachers.

The reader needs no introduction to the necessity of social action and the furthering of civil rights for all our citizens. But a reminder or two of some of the subtle influences acting upon minority group children may add to our discussion.

Two recent studies are of particular interest. The first, by Hawkes and Furst (1971), studied race, socioeconomic situation, achievement in school, IQ, and teacher ratings of students' behaviors as they relate to anxiety in elementary school children. These researchers dealt with twelve hundred fifth- and sixth-graders from eight schools representing various combinations of suburban and urban, inner- and outer-city, and public and private schools. As found in earlier studies, black children from inner city schools scored higher on anxiety scales than white suburban children. Hawkes and Furst found strong negative relationships between anxiety and IQ scores, achievement, and teacher ratings of children's behaviors.

Correlations do not demonstrate cause-and-effect relationships. They merely show that certain things tend to go together; other factors may be the causal ones. The study by Hawkes and Furst is important because it tends to discredit some of the stereotypes beginning to develop concerning racial differences in IQ and learning ability. Thus if black children do less well on IQ tests and in achievement, it is not because their blackness means innate lack of ability so much as the fact that being black, facing a more or less hostile world, they have more anxiety — which is in turn related to poorer performance. Even this statement is an oversimplification, as we shall see.

Brigham (1971) asked two hundred white undergraduates to play the part of a juvenile court judge in making evaluations of and assigning sentences to both white and black juvenile offenders. Included in the study were measurements of racial attitudes and stereotyping. Brigham found a moderate correlation between racial attitudes and stereotyping, which was also related to the evaluation of specific black offenders in terms of their "correctable potential" and to the estimation of offenders' personality traits. Estimated correction potential in turn was related to the "sentence" prescribed. But attitudes and stereotyping were only slightly related to the treatment of offenders. The judges' general treatment style was the most powerful variable in predicting treatment of black offenders.

Consider how not only students, but teachers and perhaps social workers, police, and others might be influenced in their outlook toward black persons charged with offenses against the school, classroom, or community. Might not the Pygmalion effect, in which our expectations of others cause us to treat them in certain ways, and they tend to behave accordingly, operate? In a word, prejudices affect not only the ways people treat minority group members, but the ways the minority group people think of themselves.

Prejudices do not exist only in regard to racial minorities. Historically, Jewish people have been discriminated against in almost every country. Today there is a political war in Ireland in which the opposing parties are divided essentially on a religious basis. And it is worthy of note that the entire October 1973 issue of *Phi Delta Kappan* was devoted to sexism — discrimination against females — in our schools.

THE NATURE AND SOURCES OF PREJUDICE

Bem (1970) discusses at least five sources of prejudice: cognitive, emotional, behavioral, social, and the personal.

Let us first distinguish between stereotyping and prejudice. Stereotyping refers to a set of beliefs about a group of people based on inadequate instances of information-gathering. Prejudice consists of both a system of beliefs about the group against which prejudice exists and an attitude toward that group.

Thus all Norwegians are blond, Frenchmen are amorous, Latins are volatile, and so on. The stereotype does a service for the stereotyper, since he does not have to consider the broad range of individual differences to be found in any group. In other words, it is handy. But of course it does violence to the group, not only because it is inaccurate, but because it wipes out consideration of individuals as such.

Gerald Thomas (1974) refers to stereotypes many whites have created for black people. Blacks are thought of as impoverished, culturally disadvantaged, having a deteriorated family life, and so on. On the other hand, some whites "out-black" the black in the Black Is

Beautiful vein, failing to recognize differences in education, socio-economic status, values, or morals and character.

Prejudice is essentially an unreasoned liking for or dislike for some cultural subgroup, whether religious, racial, socioeconomic, political, or other. When one is prejudiced, one resists information contrary to the prejudicial attitude. He acts essentially on the basis of feelings rather than facts. In many instances he does not realize that his prejudice exists. It may be called to his attention, however, and he may sometimes be able to modify it.

## PREJUDICES MAY BE LEARNED COGNITIVELY

Prejudices are frequently learned in early childhood. They may be modelled quite uncritically from adults, learned by indoctrination, or even conditioned. In conditioning it is not even necessary to have had experience with the prejudicial group; pairing the group with negatively connotated words may be enough. Staats and Staats (1958) paired such national groups as the Swedish, the Dutch, and so on with loaded words such as *pretty*, and *ugly* and then asked subjects to evaluate the groups. The researchers found that the nationalities paired with undesirable words were evaluated more negatively by their subjects. Insinuations and allegations may indeed be enough to prejudice one against a group; witness the propaganda of Nazi Germany against the Jewish people.

Cognitive consistency is not necessary to prejudice. This means that one may be prejudiced even though he professes a contrary set of values. It may also mean that one may hold conflicting sets of values, perhaps without consciously realizing it, possibly because he keeps them "compartmentalized," and his behavior reflects one or another set of values according to the circumstances.

Consider how some church-goers may subscribe to both the Christian ethic and a contrary church doctrine. The Christian ethic may be considered to support civil rights practices, for instance, but some church doctrines may discourage civil rights activities. A belief in "free will" may allow one to blame disadvantaged people for their condition: if they had only worked harder they would be in a better position. (Of course, this ignores the reality of discrimination in jobs, housing, and education.) Or divine intervention might be employed as a reason for persecuting certain religious groups, such as the Jews. If God has not intervened to end persecution, it must be that he is displeased with the Jews, reason the prejudiced.

Interestingly, the ministry have been found more supportive of civil rights activities than strong church-goers [Bem, 1970]. Those who belong to the church but attend less frequently may be more active in civil righ*s. It could be argued that the latter are motivated more by the Christian ethic than by strict doctrine.

It is for reasons such as these that prejudice may be considered irrational. At least it may not be consonant with one's other beliefs and values.

## PREJUDICES MAY BE LEARNED EMOTIONALLY

The emotional learning of prejudice is primarily a conditioning phenomenon. Let's assume that you have had the experience of knowing a red-haired Irish lad at school and that he has beaten you up a number of times. It does not take long for generalization to set in, and you may become prejudiced against all red-haired or Irish people. In my hometown a public square divided the town roughly in two. North of the square lived people of recent Polish, Roman Catholic descent. South of the square were Protestants of mostly English, German, or Norwegian descent. During my early elementary school days, if a child from one neighborhood ventured into the other, he would be subjected to abuse, both verbal and physical. Prejudices built up which continued for years, although they tended to disappear as one matured and interacted in a more friendly way with the people from the other half of the town.

## PREJUDICES MAY HAVE BEHAVIORAL DETERMINANTS

As Bem says, attitudes may be the result of the reinforcement of certain behaviors. This can be seen again in Nazi Germany, where the official governmental line was to reward mistreatment of the Jews. Today in the Middle East it can be seen resulting in violent guerilla tactics between Arabic and Israeli groups.

## PREJUDICES MAY HAVE SOCIAL FOUNDATIONS

Again, group pressures, manifest through indoctrination, identification and modelling, and persuasion, may induce prejudice. In high school days I lived in a town whose athletic rival was twenty miles away. When one student group attended a game in the other town, it was almost expected that fights, derogatory remarks, hubcap stealing, and other negative events would take place. It was automatic to think of people from the other town as inferior and to expect the worst from them. This extended even to some of my relatives, who lived in the rival community. It was not until college days, when I dated a girl from the other city, that my prejudice finally disappeared.

### THE PREJUDICED PERSONALITY

Prejudices are complex attitudinal systems in which the prejudiced person labels and rejects certain others; he identifies with people "like himself" and resists others who are "different." The prejudiced personality is particularly vulnerable to influence by his in-group or by persons of higher authority. He resists arguments or appeals from others who feel that his prejudices are harmful. The reasons are deep-seated and not easy to deal with.

For some highly prejudiced people, the basic motivation is really insecurity. Thus anyone who in any way threatens the prejudiced person's way of life, either directly or by implication, is automatically a prime candidate for prejudicial action. The more insecure the person is, the greater the likelihood of prejudice. Intolerant persons are likely to be immature as well as insecure, and to need the support of the in-group; therefore they reject nonmembers. Because they *need* prejudices, those who have cause for being prejudiced will be prejudiced against many people, even nonexistent groups (Hartley, 1946) and groups with which they have no contact.

Some years ago Frenkel-Brunswick, Adorno, and others studied the personalities of certain individuals found to be highly prejudiced, especially those who were highly anti-Semitic. Frenkel-Brunswick (1948) suggested that there is an "ethnocentric" type of child. He tends to have a stereotyped, rigid, and glorified concept of himself and the in-group to which he belongs. Along with this he rejects the out-group and may be openly aggressive or hostile. He rejects weakness in himself and in others, and admires the strong. He frequently is sexist. Basically insecure, he prefers a structured world, valuing conformity to accepted social behaviors. He is interested in such values as being "clean," "polite," "respectful." Being inflexible and rigid, he does not like to face situations in which others feel or act differently from himself.

One can see from such findings that at least some of the reactions against hippies, communes, student activists, and the like are manifestations of the fear among persons who see their established social order as being challenged. On the other hand, students who join such movements may sometimes do so to gain an in-group with which to identify, overreacting against the broader society, which may differ from them in attitude and behavior.

Adorno et al. (1950) introduced the term *authoritarian personality*, a concept essentially not very different from the ethnocentric personality above. Insecurity motivates authoritarianism as it does prejudice, since one protects himself through his authoritarian attitudes and behaviors. In their book, which sums up considerable research, Adorno et al. define the authoritarian as one who sees the world as dangerous and unfriendly, and therefore seeks a powerful authority to which he submits, gaining strength from that authority. Again there is a picture of conformity, conventionality, and strict morality. People are stereotyped and placed in black and white (no pun intended) categories. The authoritarian is politically conservative, preferring a strongly governed world, with which he is better able to deal.

Presumably such a personality is the result of parental child-rearing practices. Such things as harsh parental discipline, which makes love contingent upon pleasing the parents, anxiety over family status, and a family with a hierarchy of dominance all contribute to a need for "strength"; the possessor cannot accept his own weaknesses.

The ethnocentric or authoritarian prejudiced person gets that way partly by being taught. He is reinforced for his attitudes in many ways. Indeed, McDonald (1965) suggests that an emphasis on group spirit tends to reinforce authoritarianism, and Bem (1970) shows that we may change reference groups to those which support our thinking. But it is also true that the people who feel most inadequate and insecure are the most likely to become prejudiced or authoritarian. Basic personality patterns, built up over the years, are an important factor.

## DEALING WITH PREJUDICE

Prejudice is not easy to deal with, since prejudiced people tend to avoid those against whom they are prejudiced. They are also likely to resist favorable information about them. Obviously it would be preferable to prevent prejudice by teaching the equality of all people and helping everyone to become open and accepting, both of differences in culture, race, and religion and of individual differences.

When we are faced with students who are already prejudiced, however, we must work remedially if we can.

1. We can teach about the group against which prejudice exists. Menominee County Indians who were attending a high school outside their county which contained mostly white students made (among others) the following demands (Shames, 1972): (a) procure more Indian books for the school library and classes; (b) invite Indian speakers to the school; (c) sensitize white teachers and students to Indian culture and problems; (d) institute an Indian Club; (e) procure history books that present a true and unbiased history of the Indians of America. They also asked for special tutoring and real Indian counsellors (not "apples," who are red on the outside and white on the inside).
2. We can also try to introduce friendly propinquity. Unfortunately, simply instituting school bussing or using similar tactics to produce integrated schools may increase friction between groups. Preparation and free agreement to participate in such integration can help to set the stage for desirable propinquity. Often getting to know the opposite group on a one-to-one basis is more useful than dealing with groups per se. This suggests pairing of students for projects, games, and the like.
3. Role-playing and other human relations programs can sometimes help. (This will be discussed further in Chapter 8.)
4. We can talk about prejudice and the reasons for prejudice.
5. We can enlist the aid of the parents and the community in doing away with prejudice.
6. We can try to do away with minority group discrimination by enforcing job equality, equal housing, and other human rights.

7. We can try to build up the self-concepts of minority group members and instill a sense of pride in them.
8. We can build the social prestige of minority groups by pointing out their virtues and accomplishments to others.
9. We, as school personnel, can be models of freedom from prejudice ourselves.
10. We can openly reinforce those people who show nonprejudicial behaviors and attitudes.

The schools cannot do it all. Real changes must take place in our society. *But* we do have the advantage of working with children, who are often more plastic than adults, and by working through them we may be able to shape the future.

## Conclusion

Indoctrination, persuasion, and the positive use of cognitive dissonance have been described as ways of cognitively restructuring attitudes and values. But there is another side to the coin — indeed, a quite different way of examining the entire affective domain. We shall consider next the humanistic position.

Although the contrast with behaviorism will be quite evident, the reader is cautioned that the dichotomy between the positions is not as real *in a practical sense* as it seems to be. In other words, we should try not to get into a straw-man controversy. We can use something from each point of view; being carefully eclectic, we can help each philosophy to work with the other.

SUGGESTIONS FOR FURTHER READING

Bem, D. J. *Beliefs, Attitudes, and Human Affairs.* Belmont, Calif.: Brooks-Cole, 1970.
Keltner, J. W. *Interpersonal Speech-Communication.* Belmont, Calif.: Wadsworth, 1970.

## PART THREE

# Humanism
# and the Affective Domain

Humanism is a philosophical-psychological-educational point of view that is becoming increasingly popular. Although there is perhaps little scientific evidence of its validity, there is ample clinical, philosophical, and empirical experience to attest its worth. Many people find this point of view more intrinsically satisfying than a behavioristic approach to human behavior.

In humanism the emphasis is on the individual rather than the environment. Self-determination rather than adjusting to society is basic, as is attention to development rather than training. And as we shall see, there are many other differences from the behavioristic approach.

Does acceptance of humanism mean rejection of the findings about conditioning, modelling, and cognitive restructuring? Can the two points of view be combined in a meaningful way? Is either the antithesis of the other? These are questions that must be considered.

Chapter 7 delineates the meaning of humanism. Chapter 8 deals with a few of the techniques teachers can use. Chapter 9, in Part 4, deals with the training of humanistic teachers.

# Chapter 7

# THE NATURE OF HUMANISM

Here are some teacher remarks, made in the classroom, the teachers' lounge, or elsewhere about the school. What do you think of them?

"I'm going to list all the test marks on the board."
"I doubt that you should take college preparatory classes, Joe, since your ability tests are below average."
"You are just like your sister, Mary."
"I think you need help. We'll refer you to the school psychologist."
"But unless I treat them all alike, some of them will get angry."
"You need to remember that you really are quite young, so your opinions are not that great."

Each of these statements has implications for the ways teachers treat their pupils. Accordingly, there are implications for the pupils' feelings about themselves. Each statement has some implications for the self-concept, for the inhibition or enhancement of individuality, for the fostering of independence and self-direction, and for the ways a pupil might relate to others. In this and succeeding chapters, emphasis will be placed on the individual as a functioning entity more than as a product of his environment.

So far we have been concerned with a behavioristic orientation to the affective domain. Such a position is entirely defensible and earns much support from the literature and from academic opinion. But it is only one branch of psychological opinion. We shall now shift to a mode of thinking that may be found variously in existential philosophy, humanistic psychology, and especially the work of "organismic" psychologists (such as Goldstein), phenomenologists (such as Arthur Combs and Donald Snygg), and humanists (such as Carl Rogers). What do these people believe? How do they differ from behaviorists? What is meant by "humanistic psychology"?

## Semantic Problems

There are at least three prevailing notions of what is meant by *humanism*. At the risk of oversimplification, we shall define them as follows:

1. Humanism as meaning "humane." Being human and being humane are not the same thing. A humane person considers the good of the individual and also of society. He tries to deal with people in ways that are kind, sympathetic, and beneficial. Nevertheless, he may attempt to control others for their own good. B. F. Skinner is considered humane, but he is still a behavioral scientist. It is our contention that "humanistic" comes from the word "human" rather than from the word "humane." Humanism emphasizes the humanness of people rather than their creation by the environment. Accordingly, defining humanistic as humane is not really acceptable, although humanistic psychologists are certainly humane.

2. Humanism as meaning an emphasis on the affective domain as opposed to, or rather in addition to, the cognitive domain. That is, the attempt to help people know themselves, be themselves, develop empathy for others, and both accept and release emotional feelings with others. A humanist might attempt to develop dimensions of understanding that go beyond objective evidence. He might try to develop intuition, to get feelings across, to reach higher planes of understanding. This definition would include a wide variety of activities such as the use of "mind-enhancing" drugs, Yoga, group encounters, psychotherapy, and self-analysis. The humanist would attempt to form more meaningful relationships with the environment, and especially with other people. He would also attempt to cultivate deeper sensory and emotional experiences. With this may come greater self-acceptance as well as acceptance of others and of the realities of the world. The main emphasis here is on openness to experience.

   These ideas and related techniques can have real value. The quarrel with this definition is that it seems so highly relationship-oriented that it may neglect the bread-and-butter realities, such such as the need to learn certain intellectual facts, skills, and other requirements of competent social life.

3. Humanism as meaning a particular psychological view of the nature

of the human being: looking at the human organism as a unified whole rather than as a series of different parts to be studied separately. The mind and body are not separate. They are aspects of the total human being. Each part affects the whole, and the whole affects each part. For example, a headache caused by poorly fitting eyeglasses will probably also affect one's emotional behavior and intellectual functioning. One thinks of geometry; but rather than saying that the whole is equal to the sum of its parts, we might better say that the whole is greater than the sum of its parts.

From this point of view, self-actualization is the main human drive. The influence of the environment on development is minimized. Each of us has inherent possibilities for growth, and growth is a process of unfolding, unless inhibited by environmental conditions. Thus in order to understand the individual, we must study all his aspects. In order to predict his behavior, we must do the same. We need especially to try to understand a person's inherent nature; environment provides only a means to his ends — or perhaps obstacles to those ends.

Education based on this definition is aimed at providing an environment in which the individual may unfold, and at stimulating him to develop to his fullest extent in his own way. Examples might be seen in Summerhill, the British Infant Schools, and some "free schools" in this country.

Notice that these three definitions are not antithetical to each other. What might be a reasonable composite definition?

## The Goals of a Humanistic Education

*"Stand up, stand up now, Tomlinson, and answer loud and high*
*"The good that ye did for the sake of men or ever ye came to die —*
*"The good that ye did for the sake of men in little earth so lone!"*
*And the naked soul of Tomlinson grew white as a rain-washed bone.*
*"Oh, I have a friend on earth," he said, "that was my priest and guide,*
*"And well would he answer all for me if he were at my side."*
*— "For that ye strove in neighbor-love it shall be written fair,*
*"But now ye wait at Heaven's Gate and not in Berkely Square;*
*"Though we called your friend from his bed this night, he could not*
    *speak for you,*
*"For the race is run by one and one and never by two and two."*
                                                    *— RUDYARD KIPLING*

As we saw in Chapter 1, the locus of control of behavior can be thought of as deterministic or nondeterministic. Thus the behaviorist tends to think of control as essentially external. One is a product of his genes, his biophysical state, and his past learning. But the essential view of the humanist is that behavior is governed by the individual himself, who processes and selects stimuli, mediates between stimuli and responses, chooses, and then acts. This view presents us with both freedom and responsibility. And that is both comforting and uncomfortable.

The main goal of the humanist is to develop the individual to his fullest extent as a rational, moral, and humane human being. The person is to think of others as well as himself. He is to think of the future as well as the present. He is to act as well as react. And he is to accept responsibility for his own actions.

A humanist does not deny the need to learn facts and skills. But he is concerned with how they are learned, and for what purposes. Among the alleged concerns of humanistic education are the following:

1.  Meanings versus facts. That is, we might consider the following questions: "What might have been the case had the Spanish won a naval victory over England with their Armada?" "So America is a 'democracy.' What does that do for us?" "Atomic energy power plants leave residues of radiation, and must dispense heat. We do, however, have an energy crisis. What should we do?"
2.  Feelings versus cognitive responses. One wishes to know not merely his cognitive reactions, but how he feels about things. For example, consider a person placed in an interracial school setting; or one forced to make choices about a career; or someone asked to take Latin. How does that person feel about it? How does he feel about himself? About his school accomplishments?
3.  The individual versus society. In humanistic education the individual seems more important than society. For example, must a student who is capable of earning an *A* in physics actually earn an *A?* And who cares if someone cannot use correct grammar if he is able to communicate effectively? What if someone genuinely wants to study music, but lacks musical talent?
4.  Growth versus maintenance. Consider how much most of us are motivated by security, social status, or prestige rather than by more important values which may be economically or socially questionable. (This conflict will become clearer when we study Maslow.)
5.  Freedom versus conformity. How much must one respond to the demands of society? Certainly a degree of conformity is re-

quired: we must stop at a stop signal; we don't belch because it offends others. But at what point do we become merely tools of society?

6. Active versus passive learning. Much of what is learned in school is directed, prescribed, and enforced by others. And much is merely reception learning, handed out by teacher or books. A humanist wants students to study problems they consider important and to contribute rather than regurgitate.

7. Personal growth versus acceptance of others' ideas. One must think for himself, weigh decisions, consider evidence, and relate his learning to his own values. He is a growing person rather than a walking encyclopedia.

8. Exploration versus acceptance. Here we think of the possibility of many points of view on certain issues or social problems. For example, there is pressure in some schools (for example, in Tennessee) to teach the Biblical story of Creation as well as the theory of evolution. Are there other possibilities? Who is to decide which, if any, of the possibilities are correct?

9. Change versus the status quo. The world is rapidly changing; this seems to demand a person who is flexible and adjustable, and who can be comfortable in a changing world. Values change, along with information, politics, and indeed almost everything else in life. Teaching for the world as it is is not sufficient.

Other concerns of humanistic education include: knowing oneself (one's attitudes, values, biases, prejudices, abilities — whatever there is to know); relating to others; and developing one's own goals, attitudes, and values rather than buying those prescribed by others.

As is evident, the humanistic educator is trying to help the individual *be* an individual. A person should be self-reliant; he should think and evaluate and decide; and he should govern his own life accordingly. The emphasis is on developing one's uniqueness as opposed to producing a "standard" member of society.

However — and this is important — when one becomes an individual, he must live with his decisions. He must accept responsibility for his own conduct. That is why Rudyard Kipling's poem "Tomlinson" was included in this section. Individuality cannot be allowed to mean abdication from responsibility to all rules, laws, and mores, or simple amorality. Each of us has, in addition to responsibility to himself, some responsibility for the welfare of others. Humanists do not deny this. Rather, they believe that the best personality results when autonomy, maximum freedom, and stimulation to grow and develop are provided.

The humanist's position is based on the belief that people are

basically good, rather than simply the product of their experiences. Let us take a look at Maslow's (1954) theory of motivation. The true worth of Maslow's work is only now being recognized; Maslow was a major founder of humanistic psychology.

## Maslow's Motivational Hierarchy

Abraham Maslow took the position that motives can be divided into two classes: those aimed at maintenance (or protection) of the on-going human organism, and those which are growth-directed and aid its development. Maslow suggested that motives could be placed in a hierarchy from the most basic on up, and that in general the basic motives would have to be satisfied before higher-order motives would take effect. His hierarchy is as follows:

| | |
|---|---|
| *Growth-directed* | Desire for knowledge |
| | Self-actualization motives |
| *Maintenance-directed* | Esteem or status needs |
| | Affectional needs, belonging |
| | Safety needs |
| | Biological drives |

Most basic are the biological drives, such as hunger, fatigue, or need for oxygen. These must be satisfied to keep us in good physical shape — indeed, for the most part, to keep us alive. In the school setting we do pay some attention to the biological drives. We try to make sure that children come to school with a good night's sleep and an adequate breakfast. We provide recesses so they can go to the bathroom or exercise their muscles. We provide rest periods for young children. We may allow free access to the bubbler, milk breaks, and so on. Teachers can see evidence of the effect of unsatisfied biological drives on learning when sick children do not pay attention very well, those who are kept too long in their seats become restless, or it is hard to hold pupils' attention just before lunchtime.

For the most part we have fewer problems with children's satisfaction of biological drives than of other needs, although some children come to school hungry, without sufficient rest, or ill. And again, most teachers consider pupils' biological well-being, although sometimes they have not allowed children to use the toilet or get drinks when necessary. One wonders how such teachers can think the pupils' attention would be directed to learning.

Next in the hierarchy is physical and psychological safety. In most schools there is ample physical security, although extortion, beating, and other instances of pupils preying on each other are increasing. Because teachers have also been threatened, some schools maintain security personnel in the buildings. But psychological safety is also a problem. This kind of safety implies freedom from the fear of being called stupid, of being punished because one has not learned very well, or of being discriminated against because of race. The school in which children are ruled by fear and threat is not likely to enhance intellectual learning. Unfortunately, we all know of schools that are little more than custodial institutions.

The third hierarchical level is the affectional level. It includes friendship and a feeling of belonging as well as love and intimacy. Here the schools are on weaker ground. Many children feel left out or unaccepted, perhaps because of their socioeconomic status, race, religion, lack of talent, or other factors. Dropouts and truants are likely to be children with unsatisfied needs for belonging or affection. Those who do manage to find group acceptance and who receive positive regard from others are likely to develop positive attitudes toward the school situation and to make some attempt to learn.

The fourth level, the need for self-esteem or status, refers to the recognition by others of one's worth as an individual. Thus when one can take pride in being known as an athlete, a scholar, or an artist, his attitudes become more positive. But many children are mediocre or inferior in talent. They cannot be blamed for wishing they were elsewhere as they see others being praised while they are ignored. We need to find ways to help all children find esteem. If they cannot do so because of lack of ability, perhaps we can provide special situations in which they can shine. For example, a boy who is tall but rather thin may have no chance in athletics, but he may make an excellent drum major for the high school band. Another may be excellent at mimicking, although not much of a student; you can well imagine him as a comedian in the school musical production. A handicapped boy could still be able to wear a Robin Hood costume and take part in a school drama. Even without special achievement, a student's co-operation and good attitudes can be rewarded.

Up to this point we have been considering maintenance-directed motives. The reinforcers or satisfiers come mostly from the environment. The behaviors are aimed at survival in our social environment. Thus the individual is doing little more than trying to exist, and although he is responsive to the expectations of others, he has little satisfaction of his own individual wants and desires. He is essentially conforming, trying to please, and accepting direction. He is more involved with training than with education. The move to growth-directed motivation — self-actualization and a desire for knowledge — is a large one.*

---

* Perhaps the hierarchical nature of the schema needs further clarification. The implication is that the more basic motivation takes precedence over higher levels. For example, some years ago the food supply for black bears failed and housewives in the city of Duluth often found those man-shy animals around their garbage cans. (The Hotel Duluth possesses a stuffed bear, shot in the lobby when he broke through the front window.) Concern for safety, for the bears, had given way to hunger.

Also consider the conscientious objectors who volunteered to live for a while on an almost starvation diet. Sex thoughts and needs gave way to hunger; the

## CHARACTERISTICS OF SELF-ACTUALIZING PEOPLE

Maslow (1954) characterized self-actualizing people as having the following attributes: clear perceptions and acceptance of reality; ability to recognize their own shortcomings and those of others; and desire to improve and eliminate discrepancies between what should be and what is. Self-actualizers are spontaneous and natural rather than artificial; problem-oriented, with a mission or task in life; detached, reserved, calm, dignified — independent of the environment. They gain satisfaction from within themselves, experience ecstacy, wonder, awe, and a deeper appreciation of the mysteries of life, identify with human beings in general, and have deep, profound interpersonal relationships (but fewer close relationships). Maslow also found that these people have a democratic character structure; they focus on ends rather than on means; they possess an unhostile, philosophic sense of humor; and they are creative and resist conformity.

Of course, not all the characteristics of the self-actualizing person are ideal, for they are human beings too. Self-actualizing persons may have biases, just as anyone else does, and they may be impatient and display temper. They may antagonize others by their independence. They may also have their share of anxiety, guilt, and conflict.

Einstein, the Curies, Anne Lindbergh, and Eleanor Roosevelt have been considered self-actualizing. Such persons do much to move society forward.

Attainment of self-actualization is not easy; indeed, Maslow himself felt that perhaps less than one percent of the population might hope to become self-actualized. That, we think, is because of the ways our society has traditionally been structured. In order to maintain a technology such as ours, people have become specialized and roles have been carefully prescribed.

But there now seems to be a movement in society as well as business and industry to seek persons who are creative, who think and act differently from those more traditionally oriented, who are problem-solving oriented, and who can envisage a better future for

---

men's pin-up pictures were of cakes and ice cream rather than of pretty women. Their discussions were not of dating, but of meals and menus.

Yet the hierarchy is not inviolate. There have been cases of people in life rafts who gave their own meager water supply to others who were more helpless. And of course, some heroes have given their lives for others. The hierarchy is a generality rather than a fixed motivational order.

all of us — in other words, to offer more opportunities to the self-actualized person. What can we do to provide such individuals?

It is here that many young people quarrel with the schools, claiming that self-actualization is being stifled. They feel that they are over controlled, not given respect for their opinions, and are asked to conform to trivial rules. They believe they are given few experiences in self-direction or opportunities to pursue learning which they would like, but which is not formally offered. As a result, we hear clamor for reform in education at all levels.

This was our theme when we examined training and education. The schools will have a much better public image if more attention is paid to providing opportunities for students' self-actualization, giving them freedom to explore the things they wish to, rather than to prescribing everything for them.

Maslow's original formulation did not include the last level, that of desire for knowledge. However, it is not difficult to see that such desires are a continuation of the need for self-actualization. Exploration, discovery learning, creativity — such terms are used by the schools. Unfortunately, overdirection and the tremendous amount of required subject matter poured into children have militated against intellectual independence. There are many things children must learn, especially in view of the "knowledge explosion"; but schools must be on guard lest prescribed learning vanquish the desire to explore and create.

## A QUESTION

John Martin Rich (1968) raises a question about the self-actualizing individual, who may sometimes pose a problem to more conventional society. He refers to Carl Rogers (1961), who suggested that in becoming a person, one learns to feel that the locus of evaluation lies within himself. He depends less and less on others for approval or disapproval, standards to live by, and help with decisions and choices. Rich finds a possible dilemma in that the self-actualizing person, who in a sense is making his own rules, may not value the same things that society as a whole may. Being a nonconformist, may he not also be an anarchist?

The issue depends somewhat on one's definition of the "moral" person. Rich believes that "moral" people — the well-adjusted — may simply be conventional persons; they do not always represent a high form of morality. (Compare Kohlberg's levels of morality, mentioned earlier.) Thus Rich (1968, p. 118) says:

Such persons obey the laws and appear to be the bedrock of social respectability, but the locus of their behavior lies in following the group, not in making independent moral judgments and assuming full responsibility for their decisions. They are far from being morally autonomous persons.

Yes, the self-actualizing person may act unconventionally at times; indeed, he may try to change some aspects of society, as did Jesus. But he has thought through and accepted his values, and he governs himself accordingly. He is not conventional merely because it is convenient or because he is afraid to be otherwise. His moral autonomy requires a much higher morality than does conformity. Since self-actualizing people have the good of mankind at heart, there is relatively little likelihood of fostering a nation of anarchists by fostering self-actualization.

We need to be careful, however, that we do not automatically ascribe self-actualization to radicals and revolutionaries, although many of them do have high ideals and could be so termed. Too many radicals are simply rebels and are not willing to accept the consequences of their actions; too many really do fail to consider the long-term good of society. Although many aspects of society need change, a simple reaction against authority is not the same as self-actualization.

## The Self and the Self-Concept

This section further sets the stage for the discussion of humanistic tactics in Chapter 8. Here I am taking a rather phenomenological position. The term *phenomenological* is derived from *phenomenon*. This position, well delineated by Combs and Snygg (1959), holds that we act on our beliefs about the nature of the world and of ourselves, but that our beliefs are just beliefs, not actual realities. A simple illustration of this is the case of a child who believes he is stupid; he will act as if he were stupid, even if by any "objective" measures he might be considered brilliant.

Thus everyone lives in a world of his own making. Although each of us communicates with others, and although we may agree about many things, each of us will still perceive a given situation in his own way.

Until one knows how someone else perceives a situation, he cannot make valid inferences about the nature or meaning of that person's behavior. For example, if you were to see a student walking down the street wearing his hat backward, you could not understand the reason for the behavior until you had learned that the student was simply acting the clown to attract attention. Or he might, instead, be showing disrespect for the establishment; be in the process of a fraternity initiation; or even be simply unaware that his hat is not on correctly.

One may also act differently from another person, but for similar reasons. Thus someone who is worried about a forthcoming test may study carefully; another may try to sleep, hoping his mind will function better when he is rested; and still another might view a movie to reduce his anxiety.

For reasons such as these one can sometimes make quite good statements about others' behaviors, but at other times be quite inaccurate. Frequently we reason by analogy; that is, we interpret others' behaviors by imagining circumstances in which we might act the way they do. Or we project our own feelings on them and believe that they are interpreting a situation in the same way as we, although that too may be quite incorrect.

Accordingly, it becomes necessary to learn to communicate with and understand others as well as we can. Equally, we must reveal our true selves to others — and to ourselves. These goals are in accordance with those of a humanistic psychology and education.

As important as it is to accurately understand others, it is even more important to understand oneself. The self is the center of one's world, and a major determiner of behavior. Although the self includes one's body, it also includes anything one thinks of as peculiarly his; attitudes and values, morals and character, goals and ideals, and other psychological attributes.

We are always evaluating ourselves, and the attitudes we have about ourselves are called our self-concepts. One's self-concept is the result of the feedback he gets from his experiences, especially the ways he feels others evaluate him. Such feedback comes from a variety of sources: parents, siblings, peers, teachers, and others. Since perceptions of others may be inaccurate as easily as accurate, one may have a quite inappropriate self-concept. Consider the child who believes a frown from his parents indicates a lack of love, whereas in reality it may indicate nothing more than disapproval of a given behavior and have nothing to do with the love they actually feel for him. Or a child may feel inferior because he was rebuffed by a new acquaintance, whereas the other child's behavior was merely the result of his own insecurity.

A healthy understanding of one's attributes and a healthy, accepting self-concept are important to a good life adjustment and to self-actualization. If one feels inferior, he will act inferior, causing others to evaluate him negatively; and a vicious circle has begun. And of course, a healthy self-concept leads to healthy behavior and furthers the opportunity for successful interaction with others.

## Humanistic Purposes

As we have seen, humanistic psychologists want each person to become an individual in the truest sense. Each must develop his own value system and commit himself to it. He must become independent, self-directing, and responsible. He must act rather than simply react. He must develop his own goals and life style.

Humanists feel that most persons are not truly aware of themselves — what they really feel, believe, and desire. They believe that most of us live under implied threat much of the time and are too concerned with how others want us to be. Yet at the same time we may not really be attuned to others; our anxieties and defenses prevent us from really communicating with them.

Carl Rogers (1961) is a humanistically oriented psychological therapist, researcher, and teacher. He implies that many of his therapeutic goals might be worth examination by educators. Rogers sees the following changes taking place in successful therapy; why might they not also be promoted in the schools?

1. One moves away from role-playing and comes closer to being himself. Rogers implies that much of the time we act as we think others want us to act; we have been repeatedly reinforced for this all our lives. As a result we frequently do not express our real emotions; we protect our innermost thoughts; we disguise our motives. We wear masks to the world, but we also fool ourselves. We therefore need to learn to know ourselves and come closer to being and revealing ourselves.
2. One can accept himself for what he is; he has fewer guilt feelings and does not worry so much about what he ought to be. We are constantly bombarded with advice to compete, to strive, to surpass ourselves, to be like others, to improve our morals and behavior. But we can never really satisfy our consciences or live up to our hopes and ideals. Why not accept our abilities and limitations and stop berating ourselves?
3. One worries less about meeting the expectations of others and is less concerned with pleasing others. He sets his own goals after thinking them through; he develops his own value system; he tries to please himself, although not at the expense of others.
4. One becomes more self-directed.
5. One is more flexible. Unfortunately, our behavior is too often

shaped by our parents, the schools, and other social influences. As a result, we do not have enough confidence in our own way of looking at things and become rigid and afraid to change.

6.   One is more complex, or recognizes his own complexity. One discovers that things are not simply black or white, good or evil, or yes or no. One's behavior is hardly ever caused by a single simple event; rather, it is the result of a complex ordering of motives, clear and unclear; possibilities; learning; attitudes and values; and situational determinants.

7.   One is open to experiences. He accepts others and he accepts himself. When one accepts himself, he is less fearful and defensive. He becomes more able to try new things, meet new people, and accept others. One reward is likely to be that others, in turn, accept him — and that acceptance, in turn, helps with self-acceptance.

Rogers' postulates seem reasonable. They should lead to a more honest, satisfying, and responsible life, a life that is richer and more meaningful. People should move closer to being themselves rather than copies of others or what others expect. Independence, appreciation of individual differences, acceptance of self and others — all these seem desirable goals of education.

Many of the techniques we will explore next are aimed at helping a person to think through who he is, to learn the bases for his decisions, and to learn to communicate with and accept others. Other goals are to help one develop creativity, genuineness, and spontaneity. The humanist wants to turn people loose, but in ways that enhance their knowledge of self and others, and therefore in the long run enhance both freedom and responsibility. Much work has recently been done. We will see a sampling of it.

## SUGGESTIONS FOR FURTHER READING

Combs, A. W., Avila, D. L., and Purkey, W. W. *Helping Relations Sourcebook*. Boston: Allyn and Bacon, 1971.

Hitt, W. D. "Two Models of Man," *American Psychologist*, 24 (1969), 651–58.

Hurlock, E. B. *Personality Development*. New York: McGraw-Hill, 1974, Chapter 2.

Kiline, L. W. *Education and the Personal Quest*. Columbus, Ohio: Chas. E. Merrill, 1971.

Maddi, S. R., and Costa, P. T. *Humanism in Personology*. Chicago: Aldine-Atherton, 1972.

Misiak, H., and Sexton, V. S. *Phenomenological, Existential, and Humanistic Psychologies*. New York: Grune and Stratton, 1973.

Patterson, C. H. *Humanistic Education*. Englewood Cliffs, N.J.: Prentice-Hall, 1973.

# Chapter 8

## SOME HUMANISTIC TECHNIQUES

*The term* humanism *is inappropriate to a movement that does not give full priority to humanitarian aims. The family of man concept cannot be encouraged by concentrating almost all or even most of one's attention on the self. A humanist is not someone who is pre-occupied with himself. He is, rather, more likely to be deeply con-cerned with the welfare of others. The analogy to a family is appro-priate. A humanist is likely to be someone who sees all humans as belonging to a family. As with most families, when one member is ill the entire family worries and seeks to help. Humanistic behavior does not seem to flourish when a family member seeks "joy" and "ecstasy" while another member of his family is in trouble.*

*Yet it appears that too many in the present "humanistic move-ment" are, at this very moment, seeking personal pleasure while their fellow men are starving. It seems ironic and almost obscene for those in the humanism movement to justify the personal pleasures of hot baths and massages while others in the family of man are in such miserable circumstances. It reminds one of the story of two wealthy men on a massage table of an exclusive club, with one asking the other, "I wonder how the poor are doing today?"*

— MARIO FANTINI

Fantini is saying that simply being turned loose to new experiences and "doing your own thing" is not enough. The humanist must have concern for others. Black people especially are acting on this princi-ple: they are not as anxious to be themselves as they are to further the needs of black people in general. Fantini is also saying that many people who are humanists may be overlooked when we discuss humanism; thus doctors who try to improve the prenatal environment of the poor by fighting malnutrition, drug abuse, and other health problems characteristic of low-income groups; television newsmen who expose injustices; and architects, dieticians, clergy, social workers, and teachers who serve their fellow men may all be considered humanists.

We have stressed the need for responsibility (recall the poem "Tomlinson"); we have also pointed out that self-actualizing people have a deep concern for mankind. In this chapter we will be as concerned with moral responsibility and relating to others as we will with understanding and developing oneself.

## Strengthening the Self-Concept

We have already noted (Chapter 7) that the self-concept governs such general tendencies as self-confidence and openness, or conversely, withdrawing from social contact and unwillingness to attempt new things. There is also some evidence that the self-concept is related to acceptance of others and acceptance by others. Thus Maslow (1954) has suggested that self-esteem and a feeling of acceptance by others can promote kindness and helpfulness. Because one feels positively toward himself and believes that others evaluate him highly, he need not be defensive and can accept others. Those who have high self-esteem but do not feel appreciated may be hostile or resentful, as some minority group children are. Those with low self-esteem may be dependent or discouraged, depending on whether they feel accepted by others or not. Quite clearly a healthy self-concept is related both to the attainment of self-actualization and the promotion of excellent human relationships. It is clearly a concern of humanism.

The dimensions of the healthy self-concept have been spelled out as follows:

1. Clarity. One needs to know clearly who he is, what his attributes are, what he believes, and so on.
2. Self-acceptance. One needs to accept himself as a reasonably good and adequate person. Although he should realize that he can and should improve himself, he should think of himself as basically "a pretty good guy."
3. Stability. Some persons fluctuate in their opinions about themselves and are thus at the mercy of every evaluation they receive from others. One can hardly be himself if his self-concept changes with each succeeding personal encounter.

4. Realism. Here again we really need to know ourselves. Too often we have misconceptions based on misinterpretation of feedback, lack of feedback, or inappropriate feedback from others. We also may have failed to analyze certain aspects of ourselves. We may be using rationalization, self-deception, or other defenses. But we cannot be self-actualized until we can recognize our true characteristics.

Almost all the techniques for improving a child's self-concept that we are about to discuss relate to these four points.

## MODIFYING THE SELF-CONCEPT

You will recall that Maslow talked about maintenance- and growth-directed motives. In a similar vein, self theorists talk about protection of and enhancement of the self-concept. What they mean is that the self acts to avoid threat, danger, or damage. Thus if a person receives negative feedback about himself, that threat to his self-image results in a variety of defenses. He may not listen, and in fact may retreat into daydreaming, rationalizing, denial of reality, or hostility to the source of the threat. On the other hand, he may accept negative feedback as valid and incorporate it into his self-image, with consequent feelings of inadequacy, guilt, or shame.

When we are trying to change a child's behavior it is patent that we should not disparage him. For example, if we tell a child that he is lazy, we will only meet resistance. If we tell him he is naughty, we can expect him to act accordingly. There is an old truism that if we want to make a child a bad boy, we should simply keep telling him that he is one.

It is obvious that threats and coercion are poor ways to try to change people's attitudes or induce others to accept your values. Thus violent student protests frequently only increase resistance to what might be legitimate demands; similarly, cries of Black Power may only increase negative attitudes in threatened Whitey.

How, then, can one work with another person to help him change? The prerequisites are understanding, communication, and acceptance of the other person. When a person feels psychologically safe, he is likely to be more open and receptive. Any attempts to influence another should be framed in terms of *enhancement* of the self. One can accept suggestions if he knows that he is already worthy and is valued, and if there are implications that he will be even happier with himself if he makes certain changes. For example, the automobile salesman does not derogate the car you are trying to trade in.

Rather, he notes that you have good taste in cars, that you are apparently a good driver and keep your car in better than average condition — but of course, a new car will serve your needs even better. This principle seems so obvious that we wonder why it isn't followed more frequently, especially in the schools. When was the last time a teacher commented on the strong points of your term paper rather than the weak? (And then offered suggestions to improve it even further?)

Some aspects of a person are more sensitive than others; not all aspects have equal significance to the self or the self-concept. One is able to accept statements about certain views he may hold or behaviors he may employ much more easily than statements about other of his views or behaviors. For example, it is of little concern to me whether you like my taste in music, although it might be a vital concern to a symphony conductor. On the other hand, it is of real concern to me whether you think this book is adequate. Whatever is of central significance will generate more emotion in threatening circumstances than will peripheral things; accordingly, one becomes more defensive on points of significance.

It should be clear, then, that from a self or phenomenological point of view, what a person believes will affect how he processes information. Whether he feels threatened, whether communication can be established, and whether the need for change is tied in with sensitive aspects of the self — all must be considered in dealing with the self-concept and resultant behavioral change.

IMPROVING THE CLASSROOM CLIMATE

The teacher tends to set the general emotional tone of the classroom. To provide a desirable climate, he must be aware of his own feelings, and he must be emotionally able to deal with classroom happenings in positive ways. Carl Rogers (1958) long ago suggested some characteristics of the teacher that aid in producing an appropriate emotional climate. He stresses the need for the teacher to be "congruent" and to have "positive regard" for the pupil. Being congruent means that the teacher must convey his true feelings about his pupils, for those feelings will be picked up by them anyway, from his expression, tone of voice, posture, and so on. If the teacher says one thing but his expressive behavior conveys another, the child will be confused and frustrated and will not be able to trust the teacher. Having positive regard means that the teacher must accept the child as a person of worth, even though he may not be able to accept some of the child's behavior. For example, he may feel that the child's work is not as good as it might be, but he should not convey that to the child in ways that cause the child to feel rejected, stupid, or guilty.

Rogers' points are not easy to put into action, for some children are really very trying and hard to like. On the other hand, there is almost always *something* about any pupil that one can like or admire. Furthermore, one can try to view the child as a growing, developing, not yet complete person who has a potential which the teacher can help to develop.

A desirable classroom climate also requires that the teacher be able to accept honest expressions of feeling from children without becoming anxious, negative, or punitive. Children *do* have feelings and emotions, and they are real and valid. If feelings are expressed in reasonable ways, both teacher and pupils can benefit. For example, if a child states that he is angry with the teacher, instead of feeling threatened, the teacher can pursue the child's statement and try to use the information he gains to improve his rapport with the child. This is not easy, but if the teacher can think of himself as a leader and facilitator rather than as a controller, he can communicate much better with his pupils.

### AIDING SELF-ACCEPTANCE

This section is specifically concerned with children who have negative self-evaluations, either because they lack certain abilities or personality attributes, or because they think they do. Consider this short theme, written by a ninth-grade girl (Ringness, 1968, p. 342):

ME
I think I'm not very good looking and not so smart. I try to stay out of trouble, but it finds me. I am in it all the time. I would like to be a person who can be good and stay out of trouble and not hurt others. I think others think I'm a dope. They don't like the way I dress and how I act. It's so hard for me to be what they want me to be.

I would love to have a pretty little house. The house we live in is not like the other houses. It looks so old and is shaped like a barn. I wish I would look real pretty. The others in my room have real pretty hair and I don't. I'm not very happy.

It is not difficult to recognize these children. One only needs to observe carefully to see which children are dependent, withdrawing, or defensively hostile, or are fearful, afraid to try, discouraged, sullen, or "lazy." Not only what they say, but their facial expressions, posture, and approaches to people and to school tasks allow us to make inferences about their self-attitudes. (This is not to say that the teacher, counsellor, or psychologist cannot gain much insight from interviews, autobiographies, self-concept inventories, or other special instruments and techniques.)

When a child has a negative self-concept it is not usually successful simply to reassure him, reason with him, or talk him into changing his self-evaluation. Such children have had too frequent negative feedback, too many disappointments, and perhaps too much failure. The teacher may wish to be accepting and supportive, but that in itself may not aid the child in attaining a more positive self-concept. Short of psychotherapy, what can be done? The answer lies in trying to help the child to have many positive experiences *over time*. Let us consider some possibilities.

The idea has sometimes been advanced that the child should learn his limitations and be able to accept them. Thus if he possesses little academic aptitude, he should accept that fact and govern his choices in education and vocation accordingly. But that point of view has drawbacks. Learning to live with one's limitations is very difficult if those limitations inhibit activities that are important to oneself or to one's parents or peers. How would you feel if someone said that you really have no social insight and probably will never attain it? Or if you were told that you could never become a good teacher? Although most of us can accept the fact that we may not have great athletic ability, we would feel bad if we were not acceptable to others because of our appearance, personal habits, or lack of intelligence, to say nothing of such things as our race, socioeconomic background, religion — or sex!

Accordingly, I do not graciously accept the idea of living with limitations per se, but prefer to think in terms of *compensation*. There are at least three ways to compensate for a child's limitations.

1. One can try to change the environmental situation so that a limitation is no longer a limitation, or at least is no longer important.
2. One can aid the child to develop his strengths and overcome his weaknesses.
3. One can help the child to modify his goals so that the limitations do not hold him back and could even be advantageous.

Let us consider the first method, modifying the environment. The efforts of the Civil Rights movement and women's liberation are modifying job outlooks and effectively changing the environment so that race and sex are lesser limitations than they used to be. In fact, because of raised consciousness of racial and sexual discrimination, it is sometimes even advantageous to be black or a woman, or both.

Similarly, teachers, parents, and pupils can do much to modify the school, which is a major environment for the child.

Today we try to adapt the school to the pupils, as opposed to the old procrustean-bed method of making pupils adapt to the school. We prize individual differences in personality, ability, and background. Yet instructional materials, teaching methods, and even school buildings can be much better tailored to the individual pupil than they usually are.

You will no doubt be reminded of programmed instruction, film loops, cassettes, packaged instructional units, textbooks for various reading levels, and other means for individualizing instruction. You may also be familiar with modularized instruction, work-study programs, team teaching, and teacher aids. Some schools provide considerable freedom of choice of study. There are also tutoring, special rooms for persons with special needs, and more and more "free" schools. The increased use of the Montessori method and the influence of Summerhill, Glasser's *Schools Without Failure* (1969), and other efforts of the kind seem to be steps in the right direction, even though some of the steps have been faltering.

Such means may not overcome a limitation in, say, academic aptitude, but they can help to provide scholastic success. Additionally, they provide opportunities to emphasize work in subjects in which the child *is* skilled or talented. It is difficult to understand why a pupil with musical talent cannot gain a major share of his high school credits in musical activities; and the same holds for pupils with art, athletic, mechanical, and other abilities. It is unfortunate that we so frequently teach to the learner's deficiencies rather than his strengths, thereby emphasizing his lack of success rather than his achievements.

We need also to consider the power of motivation, since many motivated people achieve far beyond predicted levels. Thus we avoid telling a child that he lacks ability, not only because of the self-fulfilling prophecy implied, but because too many have surprised us with their very real successes.

Finally, if schools really want to aid in personal development, they must emphasize the affective domain more than they do. They would then permit children to develop attributes that could be reinforced and lead to positive self-concepts. And after all, in the "real world" one's personality and character are the main determiners of success.

Now let us get back to the second way of compensating for a child's limitations, developing the child's special abilities. I taught high school for a number of years and during that time saw many previously unappreciated students gain recognition and self-worth by developing their unique abilities. For example, one boy of better than average intelligence but almost no social life gained acceptance and self-confidence by becoming a chess champion and helping others to learn. Another became adept at collecting and caring for frogs, snakes, and other animals in the biology collection. Four others became interested in electronics and not only ceased to be disciplinary problems but became junior-level teaching assistants in physics. Still another boy without much musical talent became the band's drum major, developing leadership and initiative in the process. A long, skinny boy became a cross-country runner; a girl developed her voice while reading to blind students; a rather unattractive girl not only improved her appearance but became a sought-after makeup artist for school plays.

Similar skills can be taught to almost any child. At the very least, most children can find ways to develop some individuality and to use it for the benefit of others as well as themselves.

Along with special abilities, social skills can be improved. The resulting more pleasurable interactions with others can also improve the self-concept. When children are shown how their behaviors cause others to dislike them or to ignore them, and when they are given alternative behaviors to practice, they can and do change. Teachers can use both modelling and role-playing to help them.

Finally, modification of a child's goals will often help to minimize his limitations. Consider a young man of great ability who wishes to become a doctor, but whose insecurities prevent him from inspiring confidence in people. One might feel that he would make a poor physician because he could not help his patients to feel optimistic about their recovery. We might, of course, try to improve his social posture, but sometimes that does not work. But he could contribute to medicine through research, where his personality as seen by others is less important.

Similarly, one may never become a great playwright, but he can learn to be a critic. One may never play professional football but may still become a good coach. Or one may lack the ability to finish engineering school yet become a designer of machines.

This same principle applies during one's early school years. Thus a child may not be a good ball player but may achieve recognition as the team manager or the sports writer for his school paper. One may not get the lead in the school play, but he can become the stage electrician. One may not be tops in arithmetic, but one can drill himself to become a spelling champion. In these ways he finds a measure of success in a field related to his original goals, and again his self-image is improved.

## *Promoting Other Apects of a Humanistic Education*

We have seen that the self-concept is of real concern to those interested in humanistic education, not only because the attitudes and values one has *about himself* are learned, as are others, but because one cannot learn to understand and accept other people until he understands and accepts himself. Obviously teachers must direct considerable attention to the child's feelings about himself.

But that is not all. Humanistic psychologists believe that one must become an individual in the truest sense. He must develop his own value system and become committed to it. He must become independent, self-directing, and responsible. He must act rather than react.

Our teaching techniques must therefore be aimed at helping a person to think through who he is, to learn the bases for his decisions, ideas, attitudes, and values, and at the same time to learn to accept, understand, and communicate with others. *Creativity, honesty,* and *spontaneity* are terms that are frequently used. The humanist wants to turn people loose, but in ways that will enhance their relationships with others and encourage responsibility.

Furthermore, the humanist wants people to be "people-oriented" rather than simply self-oriented (or self-indulgent). That need has not always been well understood; many people have been too concerned with "doing their own thing" and not enough concerned with others and with society as a whole.

Before we study other techniques, consider the following short article (Sullivan, 1973, pp. 2–3).

WANTED: SOFT REVOLUTIONARIES

I have for a long time felt that there is something wrong with an educational system which places its major emphasis on what the teacher does, or does not do. Everything I know about learning theory or about the nature of reality persuades me that learning is largely a result of what the learner does, and is only minimally (if at all) a function of what the teacher does. And yet, I continue to hear from dissatisfied students: "I'm bored. . . ." "I don't learn anything in school. . . ." "This is irrelevant. . . ." And the responsibility for this unhappy state of affairs is generously distributed to the teachers, the administrators, the parents, and/or the "system." As a teacher, I'd like to share some of that responsibility with you. Therefore I pose this question: what have you done for yourself lately?

Fresh from the heady heights of reading *Teaching As a Subversive Activity* and *The Soft Revolution,* I am ready to give the student his rightful role in determining his own educational fate. *I* am ready; apparently *you* are not. After a few abortive attempts at allowing students self-determination, I have come to the rather cynical conclusion that students talk a great deal about "doing your own thing," but they don't want to accept the challenge of actually doing it. I recognize that students are not completely at fault; I know that it is difficult to overcome the conditioning of ten years in a system which tells you what you want to know, when you want to know it, and how you should go about learning it. But "difficult" is not the same as "impossible"; therefore I would hold you to your responsibility to yourself. I'd like to suggest some ways you might begin to meet that responsibility: (1) evaluate what exists now; (2) decide what you want; (3) do something!

For the first step, you need to use what Neil Postman calls your "crap detector." Look around you; check out what's happening in your classes and in extracurricular affairs. What does it all mean? Are you willing to make the effort to evaluate those experiences which you routinely go through day after day? Can you tell whether you're really changing the dimensions of your mind or merely preparing for the next quiz? You should be prepared to make informed critical judgments of the present curriculum and methods. But note that "informed" qualifier. Before you reject everything placed before you, be sure you know how to tell the nourishment from the crap.

Of course, crap detecting is easy, even enjoyable. But once you have decided what you *don't want*, you are faced with the hard work of deciding what you *do want*. If you want to be educated (and I assume that you do, if you've bothered to read this far), you must decide what it is you want to learn. Are there some characteristics which separate the educated person from the uneducated? If you could create an ideal educational institution, what would its graduates be like? These are difficult questions, but unless you can formulate at least tentative answers to them, you would probably do just as well to stick with what you now have.

So what can you do? You might begin by finding out what others have said or done about the problem. Read some books.* Talk to people. Find out if others here share your frustrations. Create a plan. There are plenty of teachers here who are willing, eager (would you believe desperate?) to share with you the responsibility for creating an environment conducive to genuine learning, rather than the competitive, beat-the-system, make-the-grades business which masquerades as education around here.

* *Some books:*
  *The Soft Revolution* — Postman and Weingartner
  *Teaching as a Subversive Activity* — Postman and Weingartner
  *Free Schools* — Jonathan Kozol
  *The Finest Education Money Can Buy* — Richard Gaines
  *Freedom and Beyond* — John Holt
  *Free the Children* — Allen Graubard
  *Summerhill* — A. S. Neill

*Starting Your Own High School* — James Frank
*Young Lives at Stake: The Education of Adolescents* — Charity James
*Got No Time To Fool Around* — Rebecca Segal
*Learning Together* — Elizabeth Drewe
*Youth As A Minority* — Larry Cuban

This article was chosen not because it is pushing for strong changes in American education (although such changes are overdue), but because it is one of the few discussions I have heard or seen in print on the need not just for finding fault but for being actively engaged in deciding what one really wants and actively involved in seeking changes. That activity, in turn, implies awareness and commitment to a set of values.

The number of books and articles dealing with this topic is already extensive and is growing rapidly. Discussions of a few follow. The Suggestions for Further Reading at the end of this chapter will suggest still other resources.

## Value Clarification

The term *value clarification* was given great impetus by Raths, Harmin, and Simon (1966) in their book *Values and Teaching*. Their position is unique, yet not widely different from that of Fraenkel and some others. In effect, Raths and his associates believe that a value must be freely chosen. Such choice implies that alternatives must be explored, freedom of choice provided, and the learner permitted to live with his choices. Raths says that many young people do not know clearly what their values are, and others' values are confused. As a result, some students may become apathetic, frustrated, vacillating, or in other ways unable to function successfully.

The teacher has several ways to help pupils clarify their values. Informal encounters with a pupil might allow the teacher to raise a passing question to a pupil's remark of feeling or intent. For example, if a high school student says to a teacher that he thinks he will go on to college and study medicine, the teacher might try to make him consider the strength of his interest, the worth of recognizing other possibilities, the basis for his decision, and so on. Thus the teacher might ask "How long have you had this interest?" or "Have you considered other occupations?" or even "Have you done anything about planning for med school?" I am not suggesting that the teacher cross-examine the student or hold a formal interview, but merely that a question or two from the teacher might stimulate the student to think through the implications of his remarks.

Raths et al. suggest other means of clarifying values. Anecdotes may be prepared, to which students can react in terms of their values; "value sheets," on which students are asked to react to alternative values, may be useful. The teacher may even act as devil's advocate to get pupils to consider unpopular sides to a question. Or role-playing may be used. The primary intent is to get the student to examine alternatives, to project the consequences of the position he takes, and to decide how he really feels about a given issue. He may then be encouraged to act in terms of his resultant values.

The use of value clarification techniques demands a psychologically safe classroom (mentioned earlier) in which children feel free to hold values that are different from those of other children or of the teacher. Thus the child may say that he does not value the study of a particular subject. The teacher can accept that as a valid position *if* the child has really thought through how he feels. But the teacher can also say that although the child may legitimately feel that way, a teacher must uphold certain rules for study. Lest that seem inconsistent, it should be noted that there are many times each of us must do something he does not particularly want to do. The distinction made by Raths is simply that the child should recognize the necessity for doing something he does not want to do, but should not be brainwashed into changing or pretending to change his values once they are legitimately established.

Rogers' client-centered approach (1951) seems useful for teachers who employ a value-clarification technique. The teacher is expected to feel and show genuine respect for the pupil and his views. The classroom atmosphere is nonthreatening, and trust is built up between teacher and child. Not only must the teacher be genuine in his communications with the child; he must be willing to listen to the child. The child who shows attitudes deviant from those of the teacher is not to be coerced, and is personally accepted as much as the child whose values are in line with those of the teacher.

This does not mean that unacceptable behavior will be tolerated, but does mean that a child has a right to his own point of view. The teacher, too, however, has a right to his point of view, and his view must prevail in the classroom when strong conflict exists between him and a pupil: he cannot abdicate his position as a teacher and cannot allow deviant attitudes to destroy the classroom.

Some of my work (Ringness, 1970) shows that school marks are based partly on the willingness of the child to conform to the teacher's expectations. This will surprise no one. But if pleasing the teacher is important for getting good marks, we must realize that we are evaluating not only learning, but conformity. Aside from being unfair to the child, such tactics promote training rather than education and maintain the status quo rather than contribute to efforts to change the society (school). This atmosphere is what many high school and college students are protesting: the prison atmosphere of the establishment.

In fairness to teachers, we must admit that they have developed their own attitudes and values over a period of time, and they legitimately think they have some knowledge and experience to offer. They must realize, however, that they are not all-knowing, and that others may rightfully disagree with them. The strong teacher will try not to feel threatened when disagreement occurs. He can learn with the pupils and may change his own ideas as a result of interaction with them. (On the other hand, he can stand up for what he really believes — admitting that it is simply a *belief*.) But true education will require considerable change in some of the attitudes and values of some school personnel; in fact, it might not be a bad idea to use value-clarification techniques in in-service education for teachers and administrators.

Raths' point of view is accepted by many authorities and hundreds of teachers. Nevertheless, we must remember that it *is* a point of view; as Krathwohl would put it (see Chapter 2), values may be indoctrinated, modelled, and reinforced, as well as freely chosen. Some would argue that perhaps *most* values are taught in such ways, although Raths would call them something other than values. Also, each of us is limited in his ability to accept any attitude or value; one might wonder, then, whether in Raths' sense many people actually hold values.

Raths recognizes problems in the practical world of the classroom and the school and suggests that the teacher using value-clarification techniques start slowly. He might deal at first with more innocuous issues; he should keep other members of the staff informed; and he should try to enlist confederates in his efforts. I would add that it is possible to use these techniques to manipulate pupils, and that the teacher must carefully guard against doing so by constantly evaluating what is occurring. Thus this interesting and valuable approach would gradually become acceptable to the school rather than being spurned because of the fears of some of the faculty or administration.

## Fraenkel's Approach

Jack R. Fraenkel (1969) uses an approach that is both similar to and different from Raths'. He begins with the premise that since values are learned, schools should be concerned with how they are learned —

accidentally, or as planned. Fraenkel believes the question is not, Should values be taught? but rather, What values do we want in our students, and how can they be developed? He realizes that we have a pluralistic culture; hence there probably cannot be one set of values which we all would accept. Accordingly, he is strongly concerned with the validity of any system of values to which the schools might address themselves. Such validity would be based on the *representativeness* of values, which for the most part has not been adequately studied.

Nevertheless, many of us tend to accept certain general statements as goals of our (democratic) society. For example, the Committee on Concepts and Values of the National Council for the Social Studies lists fourteen, among which are recognition of the dignity and worth of the individual; cooperation in the interest of peace and welfare; and the intelligent use of the forces of nature.

The problem is that these statements are not precise. In teaching values it becomes necessary to define more accurately what is meant and how an accepted value might be seen in actual behavior. For example, the following behaviors might be shown by a student who really valued the dignity and worth of others (Fraenkel, 1969, pp. 457–61):

*waits* until others have finished speaking before speaking himself (does not interrupt others);

*encourages* everyone involved in a discussion to offer his opinions (does not monopolize the conversation with his arguments);

*revises* his own opinions when the opinions of others are more solidly grounded in, and supported by, factual evidence than his own (does not blindly insist on his own point of view);

*makes statements* in support of others no matter what their social status (does not put others in embarrassing, humiliating, or subservient positions).

Although we do not yet know how adequately such behaviors represent the value in question (recognition of the dignity and worth of the individual), they do seem to indicate at least some progress in activating that value.

In Fraenkel's "value-developing strategy," certain instructional objectives are used to present an anecdote for the children's consideration. The character in the story is made as "real" as possible, so that children can identify with him; he faces two or more conflicting alternatives. The following plans for use with first graders is an example (Fraenkel, 1969, pp. 459–61).

Instructional Objectives. Given the information in the following story, students should be able to:

a. *state* alternatives open to Willie (the central character in the story);

b. *describe* at least two things which might happen to Willie, depending upon the course of action he decides to pursue; and how they think Willie would feel in each instance;

c. *state* what they think they would do if they were Willie, and *explain* why they think they would do this;

d. *describe* how they think they would feel if they did this;

e. *state* what they believe is a warranted generalization about how people feel in situations similar to Willie's.

Willie Johnson was in trouble! In school this morning he had thrown his paint water at Sue Nelligan and the teacher had become angry with him. "Why did you do that, Willie?" she had asked. Willie couldn't tell her, because he really didn't know why himself. He knew that Sue had teased him a little, but that wasn't the real reason. He just didn't know! The whole thing put him in a bad mood. From then on, the entire day went to heck.

In the afternoon he had pushed Tommy Grigsley in the recess line. He also had stamped his foot and yelled at the teacher. The teacher had become angry with him again. But this time she had pinned a note to his mother on his jacket.

That note! He knew it was about his behavior in class during the day. He knew that when he got home his mother would read the note and give him some kind of punishment. Then his father would find out about it and he'd really get it!

On his way home from school Willie was thinking about what his father would do to him.

"Wow!" he thought. "I'll get killed if I take this note home. I'd better take it off and throw it away."

He was just about to do that when he remembered what had happened to Billy Beatty when he was sent home with a note. Billy had thrown his note away and was sent to the principal's office about it. Then Billy was in double trouble!

"Wow." He *was* in trouble. He couldn't give it to his mother, he couldn't throw it away. What should he do? He had a problem all right. He had to make a choice, but how should he choose? No matter what he did, the outcome didn't look too good! What should he do?

1. What things might Willie do? (What alternatives are open to him?)
2. What might happen to him if he does these things? (Discuss each alternative.)
3. How do you think he'd feel, in each case, if this happened?
4. If you were faced with this situation, what would you do?
5. How do you think you'd feel?
6. Basing your answer on how you've said you would feel and how you think Willie felt, what can you say about how people feel in situations like this?
7. Why do you think people have different feelings about things?

Thus pupils are not only asked to analyze alternatives, but to predict consequences and examine feelings. By trying to empathize with the character in the story, Fraenkel feels the student will experience affective learning. As with Raths' techniques, the teacher does not moralize, nor does he foster a given alternative or value. Each child's opinion is accepted, but each child is encouraged to think and feel about the various alternatives and to come to his own solution.

## Kohlberg's Method of Moral Development

Lawrence Kohlberg (1971, 1973) has been mentioned several times in this book; you may wish to refer back to Table 2–1, pages 28–29, to reexamine his stages of moral development.

While it is recognized that various cultures may carry out moral values in different ways, their ultimate values are usually considered to be similar. Thus the school is justified in seeking to help children to move from lower moral orientations to higher. Moreover, stimulation to growth is usually necessary, for otherwise many of us might become fixated at the lower levels and never reach the higher.

In his research, Kohlberg (1973, p. 5) and his colleagues have used dilemmas such as the following:

In Europe, a woman was near death from a very bad disease, a special kind of cancer. There was one drug that the doctors thought might save her. It was a form of radium that a druggist in the same town had recently discovered. The drug was expensive to make, but the druggist was charging ten times what the drug cost him to make. He paid $200 for the radium and charged $2,000 for a small dose of the drug. The sick woman's husband, Heinz, went to everyone he knew to borrow the money, but he could only get together about $1,000 which is half of what it cost. He told the druggist that his wife is dying, and asked him to sell it cheaper or let him pay later. But the druggist said, "No, I discovered the drug and I'm going to make money from it." Heinz got desperate and broke into the man's store to steal the drug for his wife.

It is easy to see that there may be conflicting opinions on whether Heinz' behavior was right or wrong. Different people may take different positions, such as "It is wrong to steal, even for a good purpose," or "Dedication to human life is a higher value than honesty," or even "It depends on how Heinz' value structure viewed the stealing."

Kohlberg describes the work of Blatt (1973), who ran discussions of moral dilemmas in junior and senior high school classes including black and white, low- and middle-class students. Classes usually contained children at three adjacent stages of moral development; Blatt would "pit the bottom two stages against each other," and when he felt the lower stage pupils had moved up to the middle stage, he would pit that stage against the higher stage. He says (Kohlberg, 1973, p. 8):

The trouble with conventional moral education is it preaches the obvious cultural cliches. Our procedure was to throw these cliches in conflict, to pose situations where there was no ready answer, when there was violent disagreement. Only by sensing the inadequacy and conflict of his own current stage of thought is the student impelled to reorganize at the next level.

Blatt found that about a quarter of the children moved up a stage, and another quarter moved up somewhat.

## Role-Reversal

Value clarification, Fraenkel's technique, and Kohlberg's method are all essentially means of trying to get children to think about what they believe, why they believe it, and what the consequences of such beliefs might be. There is also some intent to get children to voice their feelings, an important part of the attitudinal system. More direct attempts at providing emotional experiences and understandings have included direct role-playing and role-reversal.

Role-reversal consists of asking someone to play the role of another person whose views are dissimilar to his own. As in other forms of role-playing, the learner is involved in a more realistic situation than in discussion. He is able to get the feel of how he and others are behaving and why they behave in those ways.

Sometimes the role-playing centers on a problem situation set up by the teacher; at other times the situation is allowed to develop informally. For example, some confrontation groups have tried to deal with racial relations by having black students wear white masks and white students wear black masks. Each group then tries to act as they think actual members of the opposite race might act.

Another form of role-reversal was tried by a teacher in Riceville, Iowa (*Eye of the Storm*, 1971). The third-grade teacher decided to deal with racial prejudice, which she felt the children might unwittingly have, although there were no minority group children in the school or town. Her method was to differentiate the children on the basis of whether they had brown eyes or blue eyes. On the first day of her experiment, she declared that blue-eyed children were better than brown-eyed for many reasons. For example, they were said to be smarter and harder-working, to pay better attention, and so on. Accordingly, blue-eyed children were afforded many special privileges, such as being allowed to use the bubbler instead of paper cups, having seconds at lunch time, being allowed to use the playground equipment (the brown-eyed children could not), and having their seats in the "best" part of the room.

Brown-eyed children were forced to wear cloth collars so they could be recognized at a distance. All through the day the teacher commented about the good points of the blue-eyed children and the inadequacies of the brown-eyed. As you would expect, some snobbishness occurred, and there was general bad feeling, especially among the brown-eyed children.

The next day the teacher reversed the roles. The brown-eyed children were declared superior and the blue-eyed children had to wear the collars. Brown-eyed children received the privileges and the blue-eyed ones were discriminated against.

It was amazing to see that the children's views of themselves were completely opposite to their views the previous day. Not only did the experience interfere with personal relations and affect self-concepts; learning was impaired.

Of course, at the end of the second day the teacher allowed the collars to come off, and in a skillful discussion she brought the entire group together again. Presumably the class learned something about how it feels to be discriminated against.

ABC based a news documentary on this teacher's experiment. It suggests that a creative teacher can deal with many attitudes and biases in a truly meaningful manner; the experience was much more than intellectual.

## Simulation Games

Simulation games have received considerable attention in the past several years. There are games in which a parent and an adolescent (not his child) compete against norms or against other parents and youth to gain the best scores in resolving the "generation gap" between youth and adults (Schild and Boocock, 1965). Such games seem to have merit, because they can lead to considerable involvement; yet because they are games, they may be safer than direct confrontations.

If you are interested in simulation games, you may examine them at various locations. At most teachers' conventions classroom materials are displayed in exhibit halls; most universities have instructional resource centers in connection with teacher-training programs; and games are advertised in many publications directed to the classroom teacher. (See also Chapter 9.) The effects of such games have not been greatly researched. One can write to the publisher to find teachers who have tried them, however, and thus obtain the benefit of others' experience.

In the next chapter we will discuss ways for the teacher to become more humanistic and to deal with the affective domain more openly. Our discussion will include a brief analysis of confrontation experiences, which are now being used in some public schools.


## SUGGESTIONS FOR FURTHER READING

Beck, C. *Moral Education in the Schools.* Toronto: The Ontario Institute for Studies in Education, 1973.

Borton, T. *Reach, Touch, and Teach.* New York: McGraw-Hill, 1970.

Brown, C. I. *Human Teaching for Human Learning.* New York: Viking Press, 1969.

Felker, D. W. *Building Positive Self Concepts.* Minneapolis: Burgess, 1974.

Gazda, G. M., Asbury, E. R., Balzer, F. J., Childers, W. C., Deselle, R. E., and Walters, R. P. *Human Relations Development.* Boston: Allyn and Bacon, 1973.

Johnson, D. W. *Reaching Out.* Englewood Cliffs, N.J.: Prentice-Hall, 1972.

Jones, J. E., and Pfeiffer, J. W. (eds.). *The 1973 Annual Handbook for Group Facilitators.* Iowa City: University Associates, 1973.

LaBenne, W. D., and Greene, B. I. *Educational Implications of Self-Concept Theory.* Pacific Palisades, Calif.: Goodyear, 1969.

Lyon, H. C. *Learning to Feel — Feeling to Learn.* Columbus, Ohio: Chas. E. Merrill, 1971.

Martin, J. H., and Harrison, C. H. *Free to Learn.* Englewood Cliffs, N.J.: Prentice-Hall, 1972.

Patterson, C. R. *Humanistic Education.* Englewood Cliffs, N.J.: Prentice-Hall, 1973.

Purkey, W. W. *Self Concept and School Achievement.* Englewood Cliffs, N.J.: Prentice-Hall, 1970.

Raths, L., Harmin, M., and Simon, S. B. *Values and Teaching.* Columbus, Ohio: Chas. E. Merrill, 1966.

Raths, L. E. *Meeting the Needs of Children.* Columbus, Ohio: Chas. E. Merrill, 1972.

## PART FOUR

# Improving Your Affective Competence

We have looked at several theories and techniques for dealing with pupils' affective learning. We shall now take a quick look at the teacher, and what he can do to improve his own affective characteristics.

After all, one can do little to help others if he lacks understanding of himself and his own attitudes, biases, or prejudices. He can do little for others if he is not reasonably open and interested in understanding others; if he lacks self-acceptance and confidence; or if he is not certain of his own attitudes and values.

In Chapter 9 we will discuss improving openness and self-disclosure, getting more feedback from others so that one can evaluate oneself, and self-analysis. Many of these activities *can* be effective, but one needs strength and motivation to face oneself. If we are unwilling to involve ourselves, we should stay with cognitive learning and work only minimally in the affective domain. But I think that all of us can and will profit, at least to some extent, by considering the ideas in Chapter 9.

# Chapter 9

## BECOMING MORE EFFECTIVELY AFFECTIVE

*Some men see things as they are and say, why? I dream things that never were and say, why not?*

— GEORGE BERNARD SHAW

We have discussed various aspects of affective learning and examined various theoretical views. Obviously not all issues have been resolved, nor will all readers agree with everything that has been recommended.

This is not surprising. Because the people reading this material have already formed affective states, they will evaluate what has been said accordingly. Some may still feel that the schools have no business dealing with affective behavior in a formal way; others will say that we should try to indoctrinate various attitudes and values; and still others will say that schools should simply provide an examination of various attitudes and values, allowing pupils to choose for themselves. There will also be disagreement as to how one should implement whichever point of view he holds.

Since the teacher's behavior is a function of his own value system as well as the pressures of society upon him, all that can be reasonably expected is that he consider what has been said and act according to his best judgment. He should not fool himself into thinking that he does not influence children's affective behavior, however, since even by avoiding the subject he takes a position. And to some extent he is an identifying figure and a model.

But if teachers can understand how affective behavior is learned, from a subjective as well as an objective viewpoint, they can examine their own biases, attitudes, and values, consider alternatives, and come to more carefully considered positions. After such self-examination, one is in a better position to change himself, if need be.

### Examining One's Own Beliefs

We will examine several activities in which prospective or experienced teachers may gain more understanding of their attitudes and values and of how their affective states are carried out in overt behavior. The techniques we will look at can provide information, feedback, support, and other benefits, but one's self-knowledge can really be gained only by self-examination — by reflecting on experiences, feelings, and attitudes, and the reasons for them.

Each of us probably does engage in some form of self-examination. It is useful to spend some time every once in a while in asking ourselves pertinent questions. What do I believe? Value? Desire? Are there alternatives? Have I thought them through? Need others agree with me? How far would I go to defend (or enforce) my beliefs? Do I understand how others can hold contrary opinions? How do others view me? Am I rigid? Prejudiced? How am I biased?

If you really want to go into this further, some of the following

methods might be of value to you. First, try some self-analysis. For example, ask yourself questions such as these:

1.  Am I happy here at the university (college)? If not, can I pinpoint the trouble? What does this tell me about what I value?
2.  Who are my friends? What are they like? Why do I like them?
3.  Whom do I dislike? Why? What does this tell me about myself?
4.  Which student organizations do I belong to? Why? What does this tell me?
5.  Which student groups do I ignore or detest? Why?
6.  Which courses do I like best? Why? Which professors? Why? What does this tell me about myself?
7.  What kinds of people seek me out?
8.  When I visit a classroom, what sort of kid do I like best? Least? What behaviors can I tolerate? What would I attempt to change? Which teachers do I admire? Not admire? Why?
9.  Thinking of my past history, what major choices have I made? In retrospect, were they good? Consistent? What influenced them?
10. Having a fair idea of my attitudes and values, do I practice what I preach? What evidence do I have for saying so?
11. Is there anyone (parents, peers, others) that I want to be like? Do I pattern myself after anyone at all?
12. What newspaper stories, movies, and so forth, do I get emotional about? Why? What action do I take?

You might also seek some idea of how others regard you and how they feel about your attitudes and behaviors. Generally it isn't wise to ask people directly — you can ruin a good relationship that way. And in particular, you probably shouldn't ask your husband or wife. But you can get feedback from the comments of instructors on your papers or other work, from informal advice from student-teaching supervisors, or from tests at the student counselling center — or by watching how children react to you, noticing how new acquaintances react to you, and perhaps taking note of how you act in situations that are new to you.

You can also try to understand others. When was the last time you really listened to someone talking about himself, his ideals, his goals, his friends? When was the last time you visited a new group? Have you ever attended a lecture, a movie, or a political meeting that expounded views that were contrary to your own or were pretty much new to you? When you are given some information on something, do you ever try to find out what people who disagree have to say about it? Have you visited schools in communities quite unlike your own? Have you observed others to see how they handle situations you have experienced? These questions are only starters, of course. You may have indulged in a number of such activities already; it would be surprising if you had not.

All of this self-analysis may raise some questions that you cannot answer. At this point it might be wise to try other activities to confirm or negate your impressions about yourself. A case in point is a letter of recommendation I wrote for a young secretary who was leaving to live in another town. The letter, highly complimentary, caused her to say, "But this doesn't sound like me. I'm not that good." But when other staff members advanced similar recommendations, she began to see for the first time how well she was regarded.

Finally, if you decide that you wish to change some things about yourself, what can you do about it? Some of the following techniques may be helpful.

## Using Both Behavioristic and Humanistic Approaches

As we proceed, we will consider both behavioristic and humanistic techniques for gaining self-awareness. Both should be considered. Probably the behavioristic approaches are most valuable in obtaining feedback, reinforcing attitudes, values, and behavior, gaining new information, and relating attitudes and values to behaviors. Humanistic tactics, on the other hand, are often useful for exploring one's potentials, expanding one's experiences, encountering new ideas and gaining new self-awareness, and developing enhanced human relationships. These distinctions are a matter of emphasis rather than definitive differences between the two approaches.

Obviously, under supervision, a teacher is subject to a variety of behavioral techniques for gaining self-awareness. He is reinforced for certain behaviors by his supervisor; he identifies with and to some extent may imitate a master teacher; he gains new information and may cognitively restructure his thinking; he may reduce cognitive dissonance as his behaviors become more parallel to his attitudes and values. He clarifies his objectives and analyzes his behaviors to see whether they are accomplishing those objectives. If he uses microteaching, both he and his supervisor can analyze his behaviors and gain helpful feedback. On the other hand, in loosening-up exercises, group-process activities, simulation games, and similar humanistic techniques, the education major can also gain helpful feedback, support, and reinforcement, become more sensitive to himself and to others, and be aided in making changes.

The point of this discussion is simply that behavioral and humanistic approaches have their place in teacher education programs. The choice of activities depends on one's personal objectives.

## Loosening-Up Exercises

Unlike the more stringent sensitivity training or confrontation group activities, loosening-up exercises are intended simply to help people become more aware of themselves and their physical and social environments, and to express themselves more openly and honestly. These exercises are less demanding than confrontation group activities and involve far less, if any, confrontation with others. They may be used with children and youth as well as with teachers and are said to enhance one's understanding, but without traumatic side effects. Nevertheless, such activities should be voluntary and limited to those in which the participant can feel reasonably comfortable. Experience suggests that people who willingly and fully engage in such activities gain new perceptions of themselves and others, receive feedback, use senses such as hearing and smell rather than depending on sight, and become much more aware of communication processes and problems. But some students are unwilling to involve themselves, preferring to keep their privacy; still others feel that loosening-up exercises are contrived, so they merely "play the game."

Some loosening-up exercises are group-process oriented (see Saulnier and Simard, 1973). Others are more self-directed (see Katz, 1973). Most are aimed at enhancing the prospective teacher as a person, although they are good for other people as well. Sometimes leaders are involved; at other times the groups are leaderless; or the activities are completely individual. If the student enters into them with a determination to participate fully, and if strong confrontations are avoided, the exercises are likely to help the prospective teacher and unlikely to threaten or harm him. It must be granted, however, that relatively little research has been done on the effects of this activity.

Some students who participated in loosening-up exercises have learned to put their trust in others through being in the center of a circle of others, falling, and being caught. Others have learned to make acquaintances more readily by being asked to shake hands with or speak to everyone in the group. Problems in communication are illustrated when one member of the group tries verbally to describe a fairly complicated geometric figure while the others try to draw it from his description. Differences in attitudes and behaviors are brought forth when hypothetical situations are presented, such as,

"A person walking down the street at night runs into a girl crying under a lamppost."

Perhaps you will form an informal group of your own, as many students have done; or activities similar to the ones we discussed may be part of a class in which you participate. At any rate, many of the books listed in the Suggestions for Further Reading provide loosening-up activities which you may wish to try.

## Studying Classroom Interaction

Intelligent decisions must be based upon sound data. Unfortunately we, as teachers, are not always clearly aware of the ways we are influencing our pupils, so that our decisions as classroom leaders may not always be wise. Accordingly, we need to find ways to learn how we are actually behaving in the classroom rather than how we think we are behaving. One way is to induce someone to be an observer, to record events, and to help analyze the results. This can be done formally or informally, but there are real advantages to using a well-tried and well-researched system. Of the manifold studies using a variety of techniques and instruments, Flanders (1968) is one of the most useful, and has been the basis for several later instruments and techniques.

## Flanders' Interaction Analysis

Remember that although the teacher is being reinforced (influenced) by the pupils just as they are by him, it is the teacher who for the most part sets the tone of the classroom. One therefore tends to examine teacher behavior more closely than pupil behavior; Flanders' system is somewhat slanted in that direction.

Flanders feels that teacher behavior can be broken down into direct influences and indirect influences on pupils.

### DIRECT INFLUENCE

Direct influence is a teacher-centered method of running the classroom. The teacher directs what goes on, stands as an authority figure, evaluates pupil remarks and other behaviors, and in general seems to take the position that his ideas are more important than the pupils'. He may be benevolent, kindly, and concerned, yet if he pushes his own ideas too far, his students may become dependent or even apathetic or defensive in trying to please the teacher rather than exploring their own feelings and ideas. The amount and kind of direct control by the teacher can hinder learning or even injure the self-concept by producing guilt or anxiety.

This is not to say that some direct control is not desirable or necessary. Sometimes it is useful. For handling disciplinary problems, giving structure to a new topic, or evaluating learning, direct control may be the method of choice. But when it is used habitually, direct control probably inhibits pupil growth in self-exploration and creative effort, since it causes pupils to respond to the teacher's opinions instead of helping them to develop as independent individuals.

### INDIRECT INFLUENCE

Indirect influence implies that the teacher is a facilitator, sometimes a guide, often a reinforcer and a resource, but that his intent is to get students to learn what they think and how they feel and to express it, to propose ideas and carry them through their various implications, to make their own evaluations, and in other ways to carry the burden of initiation and pursuit of both cognitive and affective events.

Flanders is concerned with the extent and the kind of teachers' and students' remarks, especially during class discussion. He does not deal with expressive behavior or the overt activity of teacher or pupils. With Flanders' method of analysis, it is possible to determine the general method of teacher influence, the extent of teacher domination of discussion, the proportion of teacher-to-pupil talk, and if one wishes to go into detail, to determine what kinds of teacher remarks are followed by what kinds of pupil remarks.

Table 9-1 shows the interactional categories Flanders has established in studying teacher-pupil interaction. Categories 1 through 4 are considered teacher *responses* to remarks made by pupils. They represent indirect influence because they do not confine the student to certain statements or questions, but rather tend to promote further comments by pupils. This is true even of Category 4, in which the teacher asks the pupil a question he is to answer; no answers of fact are required; the pupil is encouraged to state his own beliefs or feelings.

Categories 5 through 7 represent direct influence in that they tend to confine the pupils. They are teacher-centered and are aimed at promoting the authority of the teacher; they tend to shut off pupil initiation and to induce compliance.

Trained observers are required to record and develop analyses. Training is not difficult, however, and materials, tapes, and descriptions of points of analysis are available (see the Suggestions for Further Reading).

Table 9–1.  *Categories of Teacher-Pupil Interaction*

---

*Teacher Talk*
Indirect control
1. Accepting feelings: accepting and clarifying the feeling tone of the students in a nonthreatening manner. Feelings may be positive or negative. Predicting or recalling feelings are included.
2. Praising or encouraging: praising or encouraging student action or behavior. Jokes that release tension, but not at the expense of another individual; nodding the head or saying "um hm?" or "go on" are included.
3. Accepting or using the ideas of students: clarifying, building, or developing ideas suggested by a student.
4. Asking questions: asking a question about content or procedure with the intent that a student answer.

Direct control
5. Lecturing: giving facts or opinions about content or procedures; expressing one's own ideas; asking rhetorical questions.
6. Giving directions: giving directions, commands, or orders with which a student is expected to comply.
7. Criticizing or justifying authority: statements intended to change student behavior from nonacceptable to acceptable patterns; bawling someone out; stating why the teacher is doing what he is doing; extreme self-reference.

*Student Talk*
8. Talk by students in response to the teacher. The teacher initiates the contact or solicits the student's statement.
9. Talk by students which they themselves initiate.

*Silence or Confusion*
10. Silence or confusion: pauses, short periods of silence and periods of confusion in which communications cannot be understood by the observer.

---

Adapted from Flanders, N. A., "Interaction Analysis and Inservice Training," in Klausmeier, H. J., and O'Hearn, G. T. (eds.), *Research and Development Toward the Improvement of Education* (Madison, Wis.: Dembar Educational Research Services, 1968); and Klausmeier, H. J., and Ripple, R. E., *Learning and Human Abilities*, 3rd ed. (New York: Harper and Row, 1971), p. 277.

Once one discovers his habitual pattern of (verbal) behavior, he can endeavor to change it if it seems necessary. I have had some success in helping student teachers to become more indirect by first making an analysis (and recording it so that changes which occur later might be noted) and then reinforcing indirect behavior through the use of a flashlight whenever such behavior occurred. This form of behavior modification can be used to change all sorts of behavior, of course. For example one student teacher (unpublished study) habitually said "OK" to students, even when the phrase was not relevant. She was helped to use other forms of expression. Another failed to reinforce children for their efforts; the flashlight signal helped her to use praise and smiles more frequently.

Flanders' technique has been criticized for depending entirely on verbal utterances and neglecting facial expressions, postures, position in the classroom, and other important variables. Accordingly, others have developed instruments to record those activities. One is the widely known but complicated instrument, the OSCAR (Medley and Mitzel, 1963); there are dozens of others (see Simon and Boyer, 1967, 1970). And one can always build his own instrument to check a behavior that interests him.

The purpose in recording such data, of course, is the same as the purpose in recording verbal behavior: to give the teacher a better idea of what he is doing, and to provide a base line against which change can be measured.

## *Mechanical Recording Devices*

Mechanical recording devices are useful in evaluating the inflection of one's voice, its implicit feedback to pupils, and pupil reactions. The simplest device, although of course it cannot record visible behavior, is the cassette tape recorder.

Few counsellors would interview clients or indulge in therapy sessions without taping them. By playing back their tapes, they can check the adequacy of their interpretations of what the clients say, and of their own responses. They can reexamine their own and their clients' emotional tones and expressions to see if they are missing clues to the clients' behaviors. During the actual interview the clinician may be so intent on what is being said or implied that he is not focussing carefully enough on how it is being said. Or he may be so intent on certain aspects of the interview that he overlooks other important information. Furthermore, so much may be presented during an interview that it cannot all be taken in during the actual sitting.

When one has a tape recording he does not have to rely upon his memory and can replay parts of the interview as often as he desires. He can ask himself questions such as "What did the client say that caused me to ask that particular question?" or "What did I do to shut off the flow of communication?" Thus the counsellor can relive both explicit verbal behavior and the emotional aspects of the interview.

The teacher can do likewise, with perhaps the added advantage of picking up verbal behavior from the sidelines which he had not previously noticed. He can notice the typical utterances of certain children in whom he is interested — their tones of voice, the responses he makes to them, and so on. Best of all, if cassettes are saved for a time, the teacher can see any changes he makes in the ways he deals with children.

One may ask whether students are bothered by the recorder and even whether it is ethical to use one. Pupils usually do not object if they know it is being used to help the teacher communicate better with them and is not being used against them. They soon accommodate themselves to its use and after an initial period of stage fright (and hamming it up) become their usual selves. For that matter, the tapes may be played back to the pupils, so that they too can evaluate and improve their interaction.

The videotape recorder is also widely used, both in regular classroom groupings and in microteaching. It has the advantage of showing visual as well as verbal behavior, and can now be obtained in relatively inexpensive portable form. It does require an operator and some equipment, however, and unless care is used, the quality of the video can be weakened by rapid refocusing and inability to hold the camera still enough.

Is the teacher self-conscious when he employs either device? Does he become stilted? Does the lesson become formal, stereotyped, or "canned"? As with the pupils, the answer is likely to be "at first." After a few sessions the teacher usually forgets his self-consciousness and begins to act naturally.

The opportunity to share recordings with others should not be overlooked. One can learn much by analyzing his tapes by himself, but interpretation and suggestions from others are also useful. It is to one's advantage to invite opinion from others, including the pupils.


## Human Relations Training Objectives

Several states are now concerned with improving human relations in classrooms, especially in regard to understanding and working with minority group pupils and others who have been discriminated against, including women, the handicapped, and the elderly. As will be evident, such human relations training depends heavily on awareness of the affective domain. A case in point is the Department of Public Instruction Code 3.03 (1) of the State of Wisconsin (1971), which specifies human relations requirements for teacher certification in that state while leaving teacher training institutions somewhat free as to the manner of implementation.

Briefly, the requirements are as follows:

1. Development of attitudes, skills, and techniques so that knowledge of human relations, including intergroup relations, can be translated into learning experiences for students
2. A study of the values, life-styles, and contributions of racial, cultural, and economic groups in American society
3. An analysis of the forces of racism, prejudice, and discrimination in American life and the effect of those forces on the experience of the majority and minority groups
4. Structured experiences in which educators have opportunities to examine their own attitudes and feelings about issues of racism, prejudice, and discrimination
5. Direct involvement with members of different racial, cultural, and economic groups and with organizations working to improve human relations, including intergroup relations
6. Experiences in evaluating the ways in which racism, prejudice, and discrimination can be reflected in instructional materials

As can be readily seen, each of these requirement is directly or indirectly related to our discussion of emotions, attitudes, values, and prejudice. Thus, in Wisconsin experience in affective learning has been mandated and is obligatory, not merely permissible.

The institutions in Wisconsin that train teachers have been working on ways to implement these requirements. At the University of Wisconsin, Madison, major committees have developed guidelines for courses and experiences, to help teachers and students understand more completely what could be meant by each requirement. Thus, Point 1 (University of Wisconsin, 1973, p. 8) might result in a student considering some (or all) of the following:

1. What does it mean to have good human relations in a classroom? What is the relative importance, for example, of open communication? Respect for individuals? Approaches to management of interpersonal and intragroup conflict?
2. How can specific teaching techniques, lecture, discussion, role-playing, independent study, student reports, small group work, field studies, laboratory work, enhance or inhibit good human relations?
3. In what ways can human relations be affected by a teacher's approach to evaluation and grading, planning and assignment of student work, handling of discipline, interaction with parents, the use of student records?

4. How should the teacher respond to students' use of stereotypes and name-calling?
5. What techniques can the teacher use to find out the extent to which one's own teaching demonstrates respect for students?
6. How can the teacher discover the extent to which he or she judges individual students through stereotyping by: family reputation, race, sex or ethnic membership?
7. What human relations concepts should be taught explicitly? Sensitivity to others, defensiveness, ingroup vs. outgroup, intra-group dynamics, cultural pluralism?
8. What methods and materials are available and appropriate for teaching concepts identified in response to 7 above?

Similarly, Point 4 (University of Wisconsin, 1973, p. 9) was interpreted as follows:

1. Activities dealing with racism, classism, and sexism may be carried out to encourage openness and inquiry among group members regarding interpersonal relations and communication.
2. Evaluation in these experiences may center on how much the group member thinks he or she has grown.
   Structured experiences may involve activities such as the following: encounter group, role-playing and simulation, dialogue-inquiry-action group or other types of group work.

It is anticipated that a wide variety of readings, lectures, group experiences, confrontations, and other activities will be required in order to meet the needs of individual students, some of whom may already have considerable experience in human relations training (for example, through the Peace Corps, Head Start, or Teacher Corps).

In carrying out these objectives, many of the Wisconsin state universities and the in-service groups of several public school systems have relied heavily on group-process activities. This does not rule out the use of lectures, provision of information about discriminated groups through books, films, and other media, or simple discussion, but it does suggest that many of us will either formally or informally be asked to involve ourselves in some form of group training.

## Group Training

You may be familiar with T-groups, sensitivity training groups, or even confrontation groups, and you may have participated in training sessions.

With proper leadership and controls, such groups can be useful for some people, in a number of ways. With poor leadership, poor choice of participants, or erroneous goals and expectations, groups may not only be a waste of time; they may be harmful to a small minority of people.

Most group leaders believe that participation in groups should be entirely voluntary. Indeed, there is every likelihood that involuntary participation is useless for the individual and disruptive for the group. Evidence (Gilligan, 1973) shows that those who select group training are more interested in reflective thought and academic activities and are also less conservative and authoritarian than nonselectors. Selectors are more self-actualized and are guided by inner motivation rather than by peer group or other external forces. It even seems that selectors may be those who need such experiences the least, as they tend to be sensitive and responsive to esthetic experiences, to understand their own feelings, and to express their concerns, feelings, and inner experiences. They also tend to be liberal, both in politics and in religion; they can tolerate ambiguities and uncertainties; and they are flexible. But of course they can enhance those qualities further through group training.

THE GOALS OF TRAINING GROUPS

There are many kinds of sensitivity training groups, and it is difficult to determine their precise purposes by their names. Most groups are based on similar assumptions which are more or less tenable for the majority of participants.

To begin with, we may assume that even the most flexible of us may be somewhat habit-bound. That is, we tend to respond to certain stimuli in habitual ways, and our thinking may become stereotyped to the point of rigidity. Thus one of the functions of sensitivity training might be to provide models of other ways of thinking and believing or to demonstrate various approaches to social situations — to demonstrate possible new ways of behaving.

Another function might be to provide new and unusual experiences, so that one might perceive the world differently. For example, since we tend to use certain sensory media more than others, some training sessions employ the "blind walk," in which a person is blindfolded and led about by someone he trusts. Again, sometimes psychedelic lighting, unusual music, the wearing of masks, changes in clothing (or lack of clothing), emphasis on touch rather than sight or sound, or even group sessions in a swimming pool may be used. The aim is for participants to enhance their sensory intake and to attend to stimuli that are frequently overlooked. Subliminal stimuli become noticeable; nonverbal behavior becomes important.

Additionally, one should be more able to express himself to others as he learns more about postures, gestures, touch, vocal inflections, and other ways of communicating. He may also become less inhibited and more willing and able to show his honest feelings. He may become aware of the behavior of others who have influenced him, which he did not recognize before his group experience.

It may also be assumed that group experiences may help one correct misperceptions of himself and others. As people express themselves more honestly, they discover each other's masks and uncover them to show the person as he actually is. As they study others, so also can they study themselves. Feedback from various group members facilitates such understanding.

Again, one's defenses may be penetrated, and as he becomes more able to face himself honestly, he becomes more capable of change. This change may be brought about when others in the group notice his defenses and attack them. Their attack can sometimes be quite brutal. On the other hand, group members may become quite supportive, freeing one from threat, hence allowing him to examine carefully his own motivations and feelings and why they exist. Finally, group members may make overt suggestions, and even group problem-solving may take place.

Although group experiences vary considerably with membership, purposes, leadership, and other factors, Carl Rogers (1970) suggests that a number of typical member reactions and group "stages" take place in most intensive groups over time. They include tentative attempts to get something going, yet without the ability to do so, probably because of fears and defenses. Or at first there may be a real resistance to exploring meaningful ideas or feelings. But as the group become more familiar with each other and as some members become braver or develop more powerful motives to bring out their feelings, they may describe things that have happened to other people or to themselves; they may also make negative statements about the leader, the group, or some members. These statements are seen as attempts to approach their own questions about themselves, but since they are directed to others or to remote situations, they are not fully revealing. In that sense they are "safer," because the individual divorces himself from the here and now or takes refuge in attack.

Eventually some members will begin to explore themselves and to ask others for their perceptions of them; to trust others; to accept themselves; and thus to change. Finally the members of the group will become able to voice positive feelings such as affection, admiration, or appreciation for each other. In our society, such feelings seem harder to express than neutral, detached, or negative feelings (that is not necessarily true in other societies). It is especially difficult to express one's feelings about members of the same sex, perhaps because of our fears that expressions of affection may be misinterpreted.

Fortunately, it is not necessary to go all the way into hard-core sensitivity training. A number of books and manuals provide experiences in sensitivity and self-examination that do not demand as much confrontation or involvement as do therapeutic groups. And *sensitivity training cannot be recommended unequivocally.* Although most of us need to know more of our hangups and biases, and each of us should be acceptant, honest, free to explore his own feelings, and sensitive to his pupils and his colleagues, sensitivity training is not the answer for everyone.

There are reasons for this restriction. In the more stringent training groups, there are many problems in determining the effects of the training on the members. The field has been poorly researched; perhaps the most definitive study (Lieberman et al., 1973) shows that the leader is the determining factor in the value of a group — but even he may not know how or why a group becomes successful. Groups are highly variable and subjective, and observational records are unreliable. Because of these and other problems, the best we can say is that a given group may help some of its members, may be neither helpful nor harmful to others, and may even harm a few.

Every group leader tries to select members carefully, avoiding those with severe personal problems, yet most trainers have had to send members for counselling occasionally. Counselling may be needed because confrontations can cause even more damage to the self-concept when some damage already exists. Some people simply cannot bear to face their inadequacies. Other members may need counselling because of negative evaluations by the group, or for other mental health–related reasons. Sometimes, too, training is unsuccessful or may not have been carried far enough. In such instances only negative feelings may have been expressed. If members of such groups are forced to associate with each other during their everyday work (for example, if teachers and their administrators participate in the same training groups), the morale of the working organization may deteriorate. There may even be reprisals for expressed negative evaluations.

There are also problems in determining what effects of group training may be carried over into daily life. Relationships that may develop during training may not be appropriate or possible in other settings. Social climates developed in training are often fragile rather than enduring.

Another problem is that a change in feelings may not be accompanied by changed behavior. We all play roles that are to some extent prescribed by society and may, therefore, not be entirely what we wish. Also, one cannot always find ways to show how he feels. For example, the male teacher may put a friendly hand on a boy's shoulder, but how does he show positive regard for his female students?

Furthermore, there has been little study of the long-term aftereffects of such training. There is almost no information about how frequently such training should be repeated. Little is known about the extent to which people *should* change, considering stability of personality as a factor in mental health. Finally, Back (1972) suggests that the expectations of group members may be too high. For persons with real personality problems, the group "may comfort but it cannot cure."

In short, not enough is known about sensitivity training, although it has been an established technique for some time. The best advice we can give is that such training may help some people. If the reader is interested, he should investigate the experiences others have had with the leaders he might wish to engage, as well as the training and experience of those leaders. He can check with professional psychological associations, talk to persons in the field, and consult professional organizations or institutions that have held such sessions.

## Simulation Games

Simulation games are available for various aspects of human relations training (see the Suggestions for Further Reading). Because you may not be familiar with such games, we will refer briefly to one called *Blacks and Whites*, developed by Robert Sommer and Judy Tart (1970) of the psychology department of the University of California, Davis. The game is now published by *Psychology Today*.

The object is to give middle-class whites a taste of the feeling of helplessness that comes from living against strong odds. Players who choose to be black cannot win in this vaguely *Monopoly*-type game. For example, the rules call for whites to be the majority. When cash is distributed, black players get only $10,000, but whites get $1,000,-000. By rolling the dice, players move to property on which they must pay rent or which they may purchase if unowned.

As it becomes apparent that blacks are at a tremendous disadvantage, people tend to rewrite the rules of the game to overcome that disadvantage. In playing the game, my students developed a black coalition, pooled their money, and actually did manage to win.

Obviously no one can actually know what it is like to be a member of a minority group if he is not actually a member, but games such as this can sensitize people to minority group problems. And simulation games even have advantages over real-life experiences, in that one can participate and learn something about the feelings and attitudes of others without placing his soul at stake. On the other hand, when one risks little, a change in one's outlook is less likely to be fundamental.

Sources for simulation games may be found in the Suggestions for Further Reading at the end of this chapter.

## *Summation*

We have had a brief look at some of the ways one can study and perhaps alter his own affective behavior and bring his affective and overt behaviors into congruence. You will, quite naturally, favor some techniques over others. Or you may try methods that we have not discussed. But if you do somehow become actively involved in facing your own self, your dealings with the affective states of other people will improve.

### SUGGESTIONS FOR FURTHER READING

Amidon, E. J. *The Role of the Teacher in the Classroom*. Minneapolis, Minn.: Association for Productive Teaching, 1967. (Explains Flanders' interaction analysis. Also see APT catalog for tapes and other training materials.

Clark, T., Back, D., and Cornet, M. *Is That You Out There?* Columbus, Ohio: Chas. E. Merrill, 1973.

Dinkmeyer, D. *Developing Understanding of Self and Others*. Circle Pines, Minn.: American Guidance Service, Inc. 1969. (A series of kits, including puppets, records, and other materials for kindergarten and lower primary, and for upper primary and grade four, for using a goup interaction approach to developing understanding of self and others.

Gazda, G. M., Asbury, F. R., Balzer, F. J., Childers, W. C., Desselle, R. E., and Walters, R. P. *Human Relations Development*. Rockleigh, N.J.: Allyn and Bacon, 1973.

Houts, P. S., and Serber, M. (eds.). *After the Turn On, What?* Champaign, Ill.: Research Press.

Human Development Institute. *Personal Growth Groups*. Chicago: Instructional Dynamics, Inc., 1971. Leaderless group projects, with tapes and other materials.

Johnson, D. W. *Reaching Out*. Englewood Cliffs, N.J.: Prentice-Hall, 1972.

Katz, R. *Preludes to Growth.* New York: The Free Press, 1973.

Lakin, M. *Experiential Groups: The Uses of Interpersonal Encounter, Psychotherapy Groups, and Sensitivity Training.* Morristown, N.J.: General Learning Press, 1972.

Pfeiffer, J. W., and Jones, J. E. *A Handbook of Structured Experiences for Human Relations Training.* Iowa City, Iowa: University Associates Press, Vols. 1, 2, 3, 1970.

Saulnier, L., and Simard, T. *Personal Growth and Interpersonal Relations.* Englewood Cliffs, N.J.: Prentice-Hall, 1973.

Sommer, R., and Tart, J. *Blacks and Whites.* Del Mar, Calif.: CRM Publications, 1970. (A simulation game on black-white power and other relationships.)

Toll, D. *Ghetto.* Culver City, Calif.: Social Studies School Service, 1973. (A simulation game about pressures on the urban poor.)

# AFTERWORD

It goes without saying that human behavior is complex. It is determined by both inner and situational variables; by historical, contemporary, and future considerations; by physiological as well as psychological factors. Philosophers and psychologists, among others, have searched throughout history (and probably before) for a comprehensive, workable theory of humanity and why people act as they do. No such theory has yet been advanced. Each theory is subject to criticisms of one kind or another — for biases, for sins of omission or commission, for lack of predictiveness, or for incompleteness.

This should not surprise us. Man and his behavior are not only infinitely complex, but the social scene is constantly changing. At this time, probably the best we can do is to seek out what has been reasonably established regarding human behavior and make use of whatever the various theories of personality and learning can provide us. It is no sin to be eclectic if one realizes what he is doing and is not inconsistent. In other words, on the theoretical level there are wide differences of opinion, yet on the practical, day-by-day working level, many of those differences are not too important.

We have examined two families of theory, the behavioristic and the humanistic, as well as some theories that fall in between, such as social learning theory (identification and imitation) and cognitive theory (cognitive restructuring). Much from each theory can be substantiated, not only in research but from experience.

Thus, the humanist may sometimes use behavior modification techniques. Sometimes that is the only way to involve a pupil in a learning situation so that he has a chance to discover new things and make more choices, all of which may lead to self-actualization. And the humanist portrays a value system which cannot help but be modelled to some extent, and perhaps even used for persuasion or indoctrination. On the other hand, the behaviorist cannot negate the human element in determining what is a reinforcer or how the learner chooses between two behaviors that may both be reinforced.

I am asking you simply to consider whatever is useful to you from each point of view, and then to use it. When you do that, at the very least you will become more aware of what you are doing and why you are doing it. Thus you cannot help but sharpen your effectiveness as a teacher.

# REFERENCES

Adorno, T. W., Frenkel-Brunswick, E., Levinson, D. J., and Sanford, R. N. *The Authoritarian Personality*. New York: Harper and Row, 1950.

Allport, G. W. *Pattern and Growth in Personality*. New York: Holt, Rinehart, Winston, 1961.

Aronson, E. "Some Antecedents of Interpersonal Attraction," in Arnold, W. J., and Levine, D. (eds.), *Nebraska Symposium on Motivation*. Lincoln, Nebr.: U. of Nebraska Press, 1969, pp. 143–73. Comments by Zimbardo, P. G., pp. 174–77.

Astin, H. S. "Self-Perceptions of Student Activists," *Journal of College Student Personnel*, 12 (1971), 263–70.

Back, K. W. "The Group Can Comfort but It Can't Cure," *Psychology Today*, 6 (1972), 28–35.

Bandura, A. "Social Learning Theory of Identificatory Processes," in Goslin, D. A. (ed.), *Handbook of Socialization Theory and Research*. Chicago: Rand-McNally, 1969, pp. 213–62.

Bandura, A. *Social Learning Theory*. Morristown, N.J.: General Learning Press, 1971.

Bandura, A., and Walters, R. H. *Social Learning and Personality Development*. New York: Holt, Rinehart, Winston, 1963.

Bem, D. J. *Beliefs, Attitudes, and Human Affairs*. Belmont, Calif.: Brookes-Cole, 1970.

Bereiter, Carl. *Must We Educate?* Englewood Cliffs, N.J.: Prentice-Hall, 1973.

Blackwood, R. O. "The Operant Conditioning of Verbally Mediated

Self-Control in the Classroom," *Journal of School Psychology*, 8 (1970), 251–58.

Blatt, M. "Changes in Moral Judgment Through Classroom Moral Discussion," in Kohlberg, L., and Turiel, E., (eds.), *Recent Research in Moral Development*. New York: Holt, Rinehart, Winston, 1973.

Bloom, Benjamin, S., Engelhart, M. D., Hill, W. H., Furst, E. J., and Krathwohl, D. R. *Taxonomy of Educational Objectives, Handbook I: The Cognitive Domain*. New York: David McKay, 1956.

Brigham, J. C. "Racial Stereotypes, Attitudes, and Evaluations of and Behavioral Intentions toward Negroes and Whites," *Sociometry*, 34 (1971), 360–80.

Buys, C. J. "Effects of Teacher Reinforcement on Elementary School Pupils' Behavior and Attitudes," *Psychology in the Schools*, 9 (1972), 278–88.

Coleman, J. S. *The Adolescent Society*. New York: Free Press, 1961.

Coleman, J. S., et al. *Equality of Educational Opportunity*. Washington, D.C.: U.S. Department of Health, Education, and Welfare, 1966.

Combs, A. W., and Snygg, D. *Individual Behavior*, rev. ed. New York: Harper, 1959.

Eron, L. D., Huesmann, L. R., Lefkowitz, M. M., and Walder, L. O. "Does Television Violence Cause Aggression?" *American Psychologist*, 27 (1972), 253–63.

*Eye of the Storm*. ABC news documentary, 1971. Distributed by Xerox Flims, Middletown, Ct.

Festinger, L. *Conflict, Decision, and Dissonance*. Stanford, Calif.: Stanford University Press, 1964.

Flanders, N. A. "Interaction Analysis and Inservice Training," in Klausmeier, H. J., and O'Hearn, G. T. (eds)., *Research and Development Toward the Improvement of Education*. Madison, Wis.: Dembar Educational Research Services, 1968.

Fraenkel, J. R. "Value Education in the Social Studies," *Phi Delta Kappan*, 8 (1969), 457–61.

Frenkel-Brunswick, E. "A Study of Prejudice in Children," *Human Relations*, 1 (1948), 259–306.

Gilligan, J. F. "Personality Characteristics of Selectors and Nonselectors of Sensitivity Training," *Journal of Counseling Psychology*, 20 (1973), 265–68.

Glasser, W. *Schools Without Failure*. New York: Harper and Row, 1969.

Glynn, E. L. "Classroom Applications of Self-Determined Reinforcement," *Journal of Applied Behavior Analysis*, 3 (1970), 123–32.

Goodlet, G. R., and Goodlet, M. M. "Efficiency of Self-Monitored and Externally Imposed Schedules of Reinforcement in Controlling Disruptive Behavior." Unpublished manuscript, University of Guelph, Guelph, Ontario, 1969.

Groffman, Lillian. "The Need for Awareness of Values," *Elementary School Guidance and Counseling*, 6 (1971), 98–103.

Hartley, F. L. *Problems in Prejudice.* New York: Kings Crown Press, 1946.

Hawkes, T. H., and Furst, N. F. "Race, Socioeconomic Situation, Achievement, IQ, and Teacher Ratings of Students' Behavior as Factors Relating to Anxiety in Upper Elementary School Children," *Sociology of Education*, 44 (1971), 333–50.

Heil, L. M., and Washburne, C. "Brooklyn College Research in Teacher Effectiveness," *Journal of Educational Research*, 55 (1962), 347–51.

Holt, John. *How Children Fail.* New York: Pitman, 1964.

Izard, C. E., with Wehmer, G. M., Livsey, W., and Jennings, J. R. "Affect, awareness, and performance," in Tomkins, S. S., and Izard, C. E. (eds.), *Affect, Cognition, and Personality.* New York: Springer, 1965.

Jones, M. C. "A Laboratory Study of Fear: The Case of Peter," *Journal of Genetic Psychology*, 31 (1924), 308–15.

Kaplan, B. L. "Anxiety: A Classroom Close-Up," *Elementary School Journal*, 77 (1970), 70–77.

Kaplan, L. *Mental Health and Human Relations in Education.* New York: Harper, 1959.

Kaufman, W. "Do You Crave a Life Without Choice?" *Psychology Today*, 6 (1973), 79–83.

Kelman, H. C. "Attitudes Are Alive and Well and Gainfully Employed in the Sphere of Action," *American Psychologist*, 29 (1974), 310–24.

Klausmeier, H. J., and Goodwin, W. *Learning and Human Abilities*, 2nd ed. New York: Harper and Row, 1966.

Klausmeier, H. J., and Ripple, R. E. *Learning and Human Abilities*, 3rd ed. New York: Harper and Row, 1971.

Klein, S. S. "Student Influence on Teacher Behavior," *American Educational Research Journal*, 8 (1971), 403–21.

Kohlberg, L. "The Contribution of Developmental Psychology to Education — Examples from Moral Education," *Educational Psychologist*, 10 (1973), 2–14.

Kohlberg, L., and Turiel, E. "Moral Development and Moral Education," in Lesser, G. S. (ed.), *Psychology and Educational Practice.* Glenview, Ill.: Scott, Foresman, 1971.

Kozol, Jonathan. "Free Schools Fail Because They Don't Teach," *Psychology Today*, 5 (1972), 30–36, 114.

Krathwohl, David R., Bloom, B. S., and Masia, B. B. *Taxonomy of Educational Objectives, Handbook II: The Affective Domain.* New York: David McKay, 1964.

Lewin, K., Lippitt, R., and White, R. "Patterns of Aggressive Behavior in Experimentally Created Social Climates," *Journal of Social Psychology*, 10 (1939), 271–99.

Lieberman, M. A., Yalom, I. D., and Miles, M. B. "Encounter: The Leader Makes the Difference," *Psychology Today*, 6 (1973), 69–76.

Lovitt, T. C., and Curtiss, K. "Academic Response Rate as a Function of Teacher- and Self-Imposed Contingencies," *Journal of Applied Behavior Analysis*, 2 (1969), 49–53.

Maslow, A. H. *Motivation and Personality*, 2nd ed. New York: Harper, 1970.

McAllister, L. W., Stachowiak, J. G., Baer, D. M., and Conderman, L. "The Application of Operant Conditioning Techniques in a Secondary School Classroom," *Journal of Applied Behavior Analysis*, 2 (1969), 277–86.

McDonald, F. J. *Educational Psychology.* Belmont, Calif.: Wadsworth, 1965, Chapter 9.

Medley, D. M., and Mitzel, H. E. "Measuring Classroom Behavior by Systematic Observation," in Gage, N. L. (ed.), *Handbook of Research on Teaching.* Chicago: Rand McNally, 1963.

Meichenbaum, D. S. "Examination of Model Characteristics in Reducing Avoidance Behavior," *Journal of Personality and Social Psychology*, 17 (1971), 298–307.

Merrill, M. D. "Psychomotor Taxonomies," in Singer, R. N. (ed.), *The Psychomotor Domain: Movement Behaviors.* Philadelphia: Lea and Febiger, 1972.

Murray, J. P. "Television and Violence: Implications of the Surgeon General's Research Program," *American Psychologist*, 28 (1973), 472–77. *Phi Delta Kappan*, 40 (1973), 98–143 (various articles and authors).

Pierce, R. A., and Schwartz, A. J. "Personality Styles of Student Activists," *Journal of Psychology*, 79 (1971), 221–31.

Powell, Lewis F., Jr. "What Has Happened to the Old American Values?" *Readers' Digest*, 101 (1972), 170–72.

Raths, L., Harmin, M., and Simon, S. B. *Values and Teaching.* Columbus, Ohio: Chas. E. Merrill, 1966.

Rich, J. M. *Education and Human Values.* Reading, Mass.: Addison-Wesley, 1968.

Ringness, T. A. "Relationships Between Certain Attitudes toward

Teaching and Teaching Success," *Journal of Experimental Education*, 21 (1952), 1–55.

Ringness, T. A. "Differences in Attitudes toward Self and Others of Successful and Non-Successful Ninth Grade Boys of Superior Intelligence," *Final Report*, National Institute of Mental Health Post-Doctoral Research Fellowship. Los Angeles: University of California, 1963.

Ringness, T. A. "Affective Differences Between Successful and Non-Successful Bright Ninth Grade Boys," *The Personnel and Guidance Journal*, 43 (1965), 600–06.

Ringness, T. A. "Identification Patterns, Motivation, and School Achievement of Bright Junior High School Boys," *Journal of Educational Psychology*, 58 (1967), 93–102.

Ringness, T. A. *Mental Health in the Schools*. New York: Random House, 1968.

Ringness, T. A. "Identifying Figures, Their Achievement Values, and Children's Values as Related to Actual and Predicted Achievement," *Journal of Educational Psychology*, 61 (1970), 174–85.

Rogers, C. R. *Client Centered Therapy*. Boston: Houghton Mifflin, 1951.

Rogers, C. R. "Characteristics of a Helping Relationship," *Personnel and Guidance Journal*, 37 (1958), 6–15.

Rogers, C. R. *On Becoming a Person*. Boston: Houghton Mifflin, 1961.

Rogers, C. R., in *Psychology Today, An Introduction*. Del Mar, Calif.: CRM Publications, 1970, p. 541.

Schacter, S., and Singer, J. "Cognition, Social, and Physiological Determinants of Emotional State," *Psychological Review*, 69 (1962), 379–99.

Schild, E. O., and Boocock, S. S. *Generation Gap*. New York: Western Publishing, 1965.

Shames, D. (ed.). *Freedom With Reservation*. Madison, Wis.: National Committee to Save the Menominee People and Forests, Wisconsin Indian Legal Services, 1972, pp. 59–60.

Simon, A., and Boyer, E. D. (eds.). *Mirrors for Behavior: An Anthology of Classroom Observation Instruments*. Vols. 1–6. Philadelphia: Research for Better Schools, 1967.

Simon, A., and Boyer, E. D. (eds.). *Mirrors for Behavior: An Anthology of Classroom Observation Instruments*. Vols. 7–14 and summary. Philadelphia: Research for Better Schools, 1970.

Skinner, B. F. *Learning and Behavior*. Carousel Films, 1939.

Skinner, B. F. *Beyond Freedom and Dignity*. New York: Alfred A. Knopf, 1971.

Skinner, B. F. "The Free and Happy Student," *N.Y.U. Education Quarterly*, 4, No. 2 (1973), 2–6.

Sommer, R., and Tart, J. *Blacks and Whites*, Del Mar, Calif.: CRM Publications, 1970.

Staats, A. W., and Staats, C. K. "Attitudes Established by Classical Conditioning," *Journal of Abnormal and Social Psychology*, 57 (1958), 37–40.

Sullivan, Jean. "Wanted: Soft Revolutionaries," *Karma*. Brea, Calif.: Brea-Olinda H. S., May 24, 1973, 2–3.

Thomas, G. Personal communication. Madison, Wis.: U. Wisconsin Department of Afro-American Studies, 1974.

Watson, J. B., and Rayner, R. "Conditioned Emotional Reactions," *Journal of Experimental Psychology*, 3 (1920), 1–14.

Wisconsin State Department of Public Instruction. DPI Code 3.03 (1b). Madison, Wis.: Wisconsin State Department of Public Instruction, 1971.

Wisconsin, University of, proposal submitted by the School of Education to the Department of Public Instruction for implementing human relations requirements. Madison: University of Wisconsin, 1973.

Wivett, R. A. "Attribution of Attitude and Behavior Change and Its Relevance to Behavior Therapy," *Psychological Record*, 20 (1970), 17–32.

Wolpe, J. *Psychotherapy of Reciprocal Inhibition*. Stanford: Stanford University Press, 1958.

# INDEX